# Chocolate

THE AUSTRALIAN
**Women's Weekly**

# Contents

We first published this book several years ago, but now we have updated it with more of our most favourite chocolate recipes. We have kept many of our first recipes and just added some more – who can have too much of a good thing where chocolate is concerned? The only difficult thing will be to see how long it takes before they all disappear! Enjoy!

*Pamela Clark*

Food director

# Cakes

## Chocolate buttermilk cake

**preparation time** 20 minutes (plus cooling and chilling time)  **cooking time** 1 hour  **serves** 8 to 10

180g butter, chopped

1 teaspoon vanilla extract

1½ cups (330g) caster sugar

4 eggs, separated

¾ cup (110g) self-raising flour

⅓ cup (35g) cocoa powder

¾ cup (180ml) buttermilk

### CHOCOLATE FROSTING

400g dark eating chocolate, melted

250g butter, melted

½ cup (80g) icing sugar

1 Preheat oven to 180°C/160°C fan-assisted. Grease deep 20cm-round cake tin; line base with baking parchment.

2 Beat butter, extract and sugar in small bowl with electric mixer until light and fluffy; beat in egg yolks, one at a time, until just combined. Transfer mixture to large bowl; stir in sifted dry ingredients and buttermilk.

3 Beat egg whites in clean small bowl with electric mixer until soft peaks form; fold into cake mixture in two batches. Pour cake mixture into prepared tin. Bake about 1 hour. Cool cake in tin.

4 Make chocolate frosting; reserve about 1 cup. Split cake into three layers. Place one layer on serving plate, spread thinly with some of the remaining chocolate frosting; repeat layering with remaining cake layers and frosting. Spread reserved frosting all over cake. Refrigerate 3 hours before serving.

**CHOCOLATE FROSTING** Combine chocolate and butter in medium bowl; stir in sifted icing sugar. Cool filling to room temperature; beat with wooden spoon until thick and spreadable.

**tips** Cake can be made a day ahead and kept, covered, in the refrigerator.
The butter and chocolate are suitable to microwave.

# Family chocolate cake

**preparation time** 20 minutes (plus cooling time) **cooking time** 1 hour **serves** 20

2 cups (500ml) water

3 cups (660g) caster sugar

250g butter, chopped

⅓ cup (35g) cocoa powder

1 teaspoon bicarbonate of soda

3 cups (450g) self-raising flour

4 eggs, beaten lightly

FUDGE FROSTING

90g butter

⅓ cup (80ml) water

½ cup (110g) caster sugar

1½ cups (240g) icing sugar

⅓ cup (35g) cocoa powder

1  Preheat oven to 180°C/160°C fan-assisted. Grease deep 26.5cm x 33cm (3.5 litre) baking tin; line base with baking parchment.
2  Combine the water, sugar, butter and combined sifted cocoa powder and bicarbonate of soda in medium saucepan; stir over heat, without boiling, until sugar dissolves. Bring to a boil, then reduce heat; simmer, uncovered, 5 minutes. Transfer mixture to large bowl; cool to room temperature.
3  Add flour and egg to bowl; beat with electric mixer until mixture is smooth and paler in colour. Pour mixture into prepared dish.
4  Bake cake about 50 minutes. Stand cake in baking dish 10 minutes before turning onto wire rack; turn cake top-side up to cool. Spread cold cake with fudge frosting.
FUDGE FROSTING Combine butter, the water and caster sugar in small saucepan; stir over heat, without boiling, until sugar dissolves. Sift icing sugar and cocoa powder into small bowl, then gradually stir in hot butter mixture. Cover; refrigerate about 20 minutes or until frosting thickens. Beat with wooden spoon until spreadable.

**tips** Choose a perfectly level-bottomed baking tin; one made from cast aluminium is the best choice, but almost any type will work. If the cake appears to be cooking too quickly in the corners of the dish, reduce oven temperature to 170°C/150°C fan-assisted; this will increase cooking time by up to 15 minutes.

# White choc & macadamia muffins

**preparation time** 10 minutes **cooking time** 20 minutes **makes** 6

2 cups (300g) self-raising flour

⅔ cup (150g) caster sugar

¾ cup (140g) white chocolate chips

½ cup (75g) toasted macadamias, chopped coarsely

60g butter, melted

¾ cup (180ml) milk

1 egg, beaten lightly

1  Preheat oven to 200°C/180°C fan-assisted. Grease six-hole (¾-cup/180ml) large muffin pan.
2  Sift flour and sugar into large bowl; stir in remaining ingredients. Divide mixture among holes of prepared pan.
3  Bake muffins about 20 minutes. Stand muffins in pan a few minutes before turning onto wire rack.

# Mocha syrup cake

**preparation time** 10 minutes  **cooking time** 45 minutes  **serves** 8

3 teaspoons instant coffee powder

1 tablespoon hot water

3 eggs

¾ cup (165g) caster sugar

1 cup (150g) self-raising flour

1 tablespoon cocoa powder

150g butter, melted

COFFEE SYRUP

¾ cup (165g) caster sugar

¾ cup (180ml) water

3 teaspoons instant coffee powder

1 Preheat oven to 180°C/160°C fan-assisted. Grease 21cm baba cake tin.
2 Combine coffee and the water; stir until dissolved.
3 Beat eggs in bowl with electric mixer about 8 minutes or until thick and creamy. Gradually add sugar; beat until dissolved between each addition.
4 Transfer to large bowl, fold in sifted flour and cocoa powder, then butter and coffee mixture. Pour mixture into prepared tin.
5 Bake about 40 minutes. Stand cake in tin 5 minutes before turning onto baking-parchment-covered wire rack, stand rack over a tray.
6 Reserve ¼ cup of the hot coffee syrup. Pour remaining syrup over hot cake. Serve drizzled with reserved syrup.

    COFFEE SYRUP Combine ingredients in small saucepan; stir over heat, without boiling, until sugar is dissolved. Bring to a boil, remove from heat; transfer syrup to heatproof jug.

    tip This cake can be made a day ahead; store in an airtight container.

# Sticky chocolate date cake

**preparation time** 15 minutes (plus standing time)  **cooking time** 1 hour  **serves** 8 to 10

1⅓ cups (200g) pitted dried dates, chopped

1¾ cups (430ml) water

1 teaspoon bicarbonate of soda

80g butter, chopped

⅔ cup (150g) caster sugar

2 eggs

1 cup (150g) self-raising flour

⅓ cup (35g) cocoa powder

⅔ cup (70g) toasted pecans, chopped

BUTTERSCOTCH SAUCE

1¼ cups (280g) firmly packed brown sugar

80g butter

300ml double cream

1 Preheat oven to 180°C/160°C fan-assisted. Grease deep 22cm-round cake tin; line base with baking parchment.
2 Combine dates and the water in small saucepan; bring to a boil. Remove from heat, add bicarbonate of soda; cover, stand 5 minutes. Blend or process until smooth.
3 Beat butter and sugar in small bowl with electric mixer until combined; beat in eggs quickly, one at a time (mixture will curdle at this stage). Transfer mixture to large bowl; fold in sifted flour and cocoa powder, then add nuts and warm date mixture, in two batches. Pour mixture into prepared tin.
4 Bake about 1 hour. Stand cake in tin 10 minutes before turning onto serving plate.
5 Serve cake with hot butterscotch sauce and whipped cream, if desired.

    BUTTERSCOTCH SAUCE Combine ingredients in saucepan; stir over heat, without boiling, until sugar is dissolved. Simmer, without stirring, 3 minutes.

cakes

# Chocolate roulade with coffee cream

**preparation time** 20 minutes (plus cooling and chilling time)  **cooking time** 10 minutes  **serves** 8

1 tablespoon caster sugar

200g dark cooking chocolate, chopped coarsely

¼ cup (60ml) hot water

1 tablespoon instant coffee powder

4 eggs, separated

½ cup (110g) caster sugar, extra

1 teaspoon hot water, extra

300ml whipping cream

2 tablespoons coffee-flavoured liqueur

1 tablespoon icing sugar

1  Preheat oven to 180°C/160°C fan-assisted. Grease 25cm x 30cm swiss roll tin; line base with baking parchment. Place a piece of baking parchment cut the same size as swiss roll tin on board or bench; sprinkle evenly with caster sugar.

2  Combine chocolate, the water and half of the coffee powder in large heatproof bowl. Stir over large saucepan of simmering water until smooth; remove from heat.

3  Beat egg yolks and extra caster sugar in small bowl with electric mixer until thick and creamy; fold egg mixture into warm chocolate mixture.

4  Meanwhile, beat egg whites in clean small bowl with electric mixer until soft peaks form; fold egg whites, in two batches, into chocolate mixture. Spread into prepared tin; bake cake about 10 minutes.

5  Turn cake onto sugared paper, peel baking parchment away; use serrated knife to cut away crisp edges from all sides. Cover cake with tea towel; cool.

6  Dissolve remaining coffee powder in the extra water in small bowl. Add cream, liqueur and icing sugar; beat with electric mixer until firm peaks form. Spread cake evenly with cream mixture. Roll cake, from long side, by lifting paper and using it to guide the roll into shape. Cover roll; refrigerate 30 minutes before serving.

**tip**  Be sure you beat the egg yolk mixture until thick, and the egg whites only until soft peaks form. Overbeating will dry out the egg whites and make them difficult to fold into the chocolate mixture.

# White chocolate mud cake

preparation time 50 minutes (plus cooling time)  cooking time 1 hour 45 minutes  serves 12

250g butter, chopped

180g white eating chocolate, chopped coarsely

1½ cups (330g) caster sugar

¾ cup (180ml) milk

1½ cups (225g) plain flour

½ cup (75g) self-raising flour

½ teaspoon vanilla extract

2 eggs, beaten lightly

WHITE CHOCOLATE GANACHE

½ cup (125ml) whipping cream

360g white eating chocolate, chopped finely

1 Preheat oven to 170°C/150°C fan-assisted Grease deep 20cm-round cake tin; line base and side with baking parchment.

2 Combine butter, chocolate, sugar and milk in medium saucepan; stir over low heat until melted. Transfer mixture to large bowl; cool 15 minutes.

3 Stir in sifted flours, extract and egg; pour into prepared tin. Bake, uncovered, about 1 hour 40 minutes; cool cake in tin.

4 Meanwhile, make white chocolate ganache.

5 Turn cake onto serving plate top-side up. Spread ganache all over cake; top with chocolate curls, if desired.

WHITE CHOCOLATE GANACHE Bring cream to a boil in small pan; pour over chocolate in heatproof bowl, stir with wooden spoon until chocolate melts. Cover bowl; refrigerate, stirring occasionally, about 30 minutes or until ganache is of a spreadable consistency.

# Double-decker mud cake

preparation time 30 minutes (plus cooling time)  cooking time 1 hour  serves 10

250g butter, chopped

150g white cooking chocolate, chopped coarsely

2 cups (440g) caster sugar

1 cup (250ml) milk

1½ cups (225g) plain flour

½ cup (75g) self-raising flour

1 teaspoon vanilla essence

2 eggs, beaten lightly

2 tablespoons cocoa powder

MILK CHOCOLATE GANACHE

600g milk cooking chocolate, chopped coarsely

1 cup (250ml) double cream

1 Preheat oven to 150°C.130°C fan-assisted. Grease two deep 20cm-round cake tins; line bases and sides with baking parchment.

2 Combine butter, white chocolate, sugar and milk in medium saucepan; stir over heat, without boiling, until smooth. Transfer mixture to large bowl; cool 15 minutes.

3 Whisk sifted flours into white chocolate mixture, then whisk in essence and egg; pour half of the mixture into one of the prepared tins. Whisk sifted cocoa into remaining mixture; pour into other prepared tin. Bake cakes about 50 minutes. Stand cakes in tins 5 minutes; turn cakes, top-side up, onto wire rack to cool.

4 Meanwhile, make milk chocolate ganache. Reserve 1 cup of ganache for spreading over cake.

5 Split each cooled cake in half. Centre one layer of cake on serving plate; spread with ½ cup of the remaining milk chocolate mixture. Repeat layering, alternating colours. Cover top and sides of cake with reserved milk chocolate mixture.

MILK CHOCOLATE GANACHE Combine chocolate and cream in medium pan; stir over low heat until smooth. Transfer to medium bowl. Cover; refrigerate, stirring occasionally, until spreadable.

tip You can also melt the milk chocolate and cream in a microwave oven; cook on high (100%) about 1½ minutes, pausing to stir every 30 seconds.

cakes

# Low-fat chocolate fudge cake

**preparation time** 20 minutes  **cooking time** 40 minutes  **serves** 8

85g dark eating chocolate, chopped finely

½ cup (50g) cocoa powder

1 cup (200g) firmly packed brown sugar

½ cup (125ml) boiling water

2 egg yolks

¼ cup (30g) ground almonds

⅓ cup (50g) wholemeal plain flour

4 egg whites

1 Preheat oven to 180°C/160°C fan-assisted. Line base and side of deep 20cm-round cake tin with baking parchment.

2 Combine chocolate, cocoa and sugar with the water in large bowl; stir until smooth. Add egg yolks; whisk to combine. Fold in ground almonds and flour.

3 Beat egg whites in small bowl with electric mixer until firm peaks form. Gently fold egg white mixture into chocolate mixture, in two batches; pour into prepared tin.

4 Bake in cake about 40 minutes. Stand in tin 5 minutes, then turn onto wire rack; remove paper.

**tip** Serve warm, dusted with icing sugar and topped with strawberries.

# Rich chocolate meringue cake

**preparation time** 15 minutes  **cooking time** 1 hour 30 minutes  **serves** 8

8 egg whites

1 cup (220g) caster sugar

60g dark cooking chocolate, chopped finely

¼ cup (60g) finely chopped glacé figs

¼ cup (50g) finely chopped pitted prunes

¾ cup (45g) stale breadcrumbs

¼ cup (25g) cocoa powder

1 tablespoon icing sugar

1 tablespoon cocoa powder, extra

1 Preheat oven to 120°C/110°C fan-assisted. Grease 22cm springform tin; line base and side with baking parchment.

2 Beat egg whites in medium bowl with electric mixer until soft peaks form. Add sugar, 1 tablespoon at a time, beating until sugar dissolves between each addition. Fold in chocolate, fruit, breadcrumbs and sifted cocoa.

3 Spoon mixture into prepared tin; bake cake 1½ hours. Cool in oven with door ajar.

4 Dust with combined sifted icing sugar and extra cocoa; serve with whipped cream, if desired.

**tip** Serve with fresh strawberries or cherries, if desired.

# Sacher torte

**preparation time** 30 minutes (plus standing and cooling time) **cooking time** 30 minutes **serves** 10 to 12

150g dark eating chocolate, chopped

1 tablespoon warm water

150g butter, chopped

½ cup (110g) caster sugar

3 eggs, separated

1 cup (150g) plain flour

2 tablespoons caster sugar, extra

⅔ cup (220g) apricot jam

CHOCOLATE ICING

125g dark eating chocolate, chopped

125g butter

1 Preheat oven to 180°C/160°C fan-assisted. Grease deep 22cm-round cake tin; line base with baking parchment.

2 Melt chocolate in heatproof bowl over hot water, stir in the water; cool to room temperature.

3 Beat butter and sugar in small bowl with electric mixer until pale in colour. Beat in egg yolks one at a time, until combined between each addition. Transfer mixture to large bowl; stir in chocolate mixture, then sifted flour.

4 Beat egg whites in clean small bowl until soft peaks form, gradually add extra sugar, beat until dissolved between each addition; fold lightly into chocolate mixture. Spread mixture into prepared tin.

5 Bake about 30 minutes. Stand cake in tin 5 minutes before turning onto wire rack to cool; leave cake upside down to cool.

6 Split cake in half, place one half on serving plate. Heat and strain jam, brush over half of the cake. Top with remaining half of cake, brush cake all over with remaining jam. Stand about 1 hour at room temperature to allow jam to set. Make chocolate icing.

7 Spread top and side of cake with chocolate icing; set at room temperature.
CHOCOLATE ICING Melt chocolate and butter in medium bowl over hot water, stir until smooth. Cool to room temperature until spreadable, stir occasionally; this can take up to 2 hours.

tip This icing is also suitable for piping.

# Upside-down choc-caramel nut cake

**preparation time** 15 minutes **cooking time** 1 hour 20 minutes **serves** 10

2 tablespoons chopped, toasted macadamias

2 tablespoons chopped, toasted pistachios

2 tablespoons chopped, toasted walnuts

125g butter, chopped

1 cup (220g) firmly packed brown sugar

3 eggs

1 cup (150g) self-raising flour

¼ cup (35g) plain flour

¼ teaspoon bicarbonate of soda

⅓ cup (35g) cocoa powder

100g dark eating chocolate, melted

¾ cup (180ml) milk

CARAMEL TOPPING

40g butter

¼ cup (55g) firmly packed brown sugar

2 tablespoons double cream

1 Preheat oven to 170°C/150°C fan-assisted. Grease deep 20cm-round cake tin; line base with baking parchment.

2 Make caramel topping. Pour hot topping over base of prepared tin, sprinkle combined nuts over caramel; freeze while preparing cake mixture.

3 Beat butter and sugar in small bowl with electric mixer until light and fluffy. Beat in eggs, one at a time, until just combined between each addition.

4 Stir in sifted flours, bicarbonate of soda and cocoa powder, then chocolate and milk. Spread cake mixture over caramel nut topping.

5 Bake about 1 hour 10 minutes. Stand cake in tin 15 minutes before turning onto wire rack to cool.
CARAMEL TOPPING Combine butter, sugar and cream in small saucepan; stir over low heat, without boiling, until sugar is dissolved. Bring to a boil, then remove from heat.

**tips** This cake can be made a day ahead and kept in an airtight container. Use unsalted nuts.

# Gluten-free chocolate cake

**preparation time** 20 minutes (plus cooling time) **cooking time** 30 minutes **serves** 8

*You will need one large (230g) overripe banana for this recipe.*

1 cup (125g) soy flour

¾ cup (110g) cornflour

1¼ teaspoons bicarbonate of soda

½ cup (50g) cocoa powder

1¼ cups (275g) caster sugar

150g butter, melted

1 tablespoon white vinegar

1 cup (250ml) evaporated milk

2 eggs

½ cup mashed banana

2 tablespoons raspberry jam

300ml whipping cream

1 Preheat oven to 180°C/160°C fan-assisted. Grease two 22cm-round sandwich cake tins; line bases with baking parchment.

2 Sift flours, bicarbonate of soda, cocoa and sugar into large bowl; add butter, vinegar and milk. Beat with electric mixer on low speed 1 minute; add eggs, banana and jam, beat on medium speed 2 minutes. Pour mixture into prepared tins.

3 Bake about 30 minutes. Stand cakes in tins 5 minutes before turning onto wire racks to cool.

4 Beat cream in small bowl with electric mixer until firm peaks form. Sandwich cakes with whipped cream; lightly dust with sifted icing sugar or sifted cocoa, if desired.

**tips** Store unfilled cakes in airtight containers for up to two days. Sandwich cake with whipped cream close to serving. Cake not suitable to freeze.

# Irish cream & chocolate mousse cake

**preparation time** 30 minutes (plus cooling and refrigeration time) **cooking time** 15 minutes **serves** 12

6 eggs, separated

½ cup (80g) icing sugar

¼ cup (25g) cocoa powder

2 tablespoons cornflour

150g dark eating chocolate, melted

1 tablespoon water

600ml double cream

450g dark eating chocolate, chopped coarsely, extra

¾ cup (180ml) irish cream liqueur

1 tablespoon cocoa powder, extra

1  Preheat oven to 180°C/160°C fan-assisted. Grease 25cm x 30cm swiss roll tin; line base and sides with baking parchment.

2  Beat egg yolks and icing sugar in small bowl with electric mixer until thick and creamy; transfer to large bowl. Fold in combined sifted cocoa and cornflour, then chocolate; fold in the water.

3  Beat egg whites in medium bowl with electric mixer until soft peaks form. Fold egg whites, in two batches, into chocolate mixture. Spread mixture into prepared tin; bake cake about 15 minutes. Turn cake onto baking-parchment-covered wire rack. Cover cake with baking parchment; cool to room temperature.

4  Grease 22cm springform tin; line side with baking parchment, bringing paper 5cm above edge of tin. Cut 22cm-diameter circle from cooled cake; place in prepared tin. Discard remaining cake.

5  Combine cream and extra chocolate in medium saucepan; stir over low heat until smooth. Transfer to large bowl; refrigerate until just cold.

6  Add liqueur to chocolate mixture; beat with electric mixer until mixture changes to a paler colour. Pour mixture into prepared tin; refrigerate about 3 hours or until set.

7  Transfer cake from tin to serving plate; dust with sifted extra cocoa.

**tip** Do not overbeat the chocolate and liqueur mixture as it will curdle.

# Mini choc chip almond cakes

**preparation time** 20 minutes  **cooking time** 20 minutes  **makes** 18

3 egg whites
90g butter, melted
½ cup (60g) ground almonds
¾ cup (120g) icing sugar
¼ cup (35g) plain flour
100g dark eating chocolate, chopped finely
¼ cup (60ml) double cream
100g dark eating chocolate, chopped, extra

1  Preheat oven to 180°C/160°C fan-assisted. Grease 2 x 12-hole mini muffin pans.
2  Place egg whites in medium bowl; whisk lightly with a fork until combined. Add butter, ground almonds and sifted icing sugar and flour; using a wooden spoon, stir until just combined. Stir in finely chopped chocolate. Spoon tablespoons of mixture into prepared pan holes. Bake about 15 minutes or until browned lightly and cooked through. Turn onto wire racks to cool.
3  Combine cream and extra chocolate in a medium heatproof bowl over a pan of simmering water; stir until just melted. Stand until thickened. Spoon chocolate mixture over tops of almond cakes.

**tips** This recipe can be made a day ahead. Almond cakes are suitable to freeze.
Chocolate mixture is suitable to microwave.

# Warm chocolate polenta cakes with chocolate sauce

**preparation time** 20 minutes  **cooking time** 30 minutes  **makes** 8

125g softened butter
⅔ cup (150g) caster sugar
1¼ cups (150g) ground almonds
¼ cup (25g) cocoa powder
50g dark eating chocolate, grated
2 eggs
½ cup (85g) instant polenta
⅓ cup (80ml) milk

CHOCOLATE SAUCE
125g dark eating chocolate, chopped
½ cup (125ml) double cream

1  Preheat oven to 170°C/150°C fan-assisted. Grease 8 holes of two large (⅓-cup/80ml) muffin pans, line the bases with baking parchment.
2  Beat butter and sugar in a small bowl with an electric mixer until light and fluffy. Add ground almonds, sifted cocoa and chocolate, mix until just combined. Add eggs one at a time, beating well between additions. Stir in combined polenta and milk.
3  Divide mixture among prepared tins. Bake about 30 minutes or until cooked when tested. Turn onto a wire rack to cool slightly. Make chocolate sauce; serve with warm cakes.
CHOCOLATE SAUCE Combine chocolate and cream in a heatproof bowl; stir over a pan of simmering water until melted.

**tips** This recipe can be made a day ahead. Cakes are suitable to freeze. Sauce is suitable to microwave.

# Dark chocolate and almond torte

**preparation time** 20 minutes (plus standing time) **cooking time** 55 minutes **serves** 14

*Caramelised almonds are whole almonds coated in toffee. They are available from selected supermarkets, nut shops and gourmet food and specialty confectionery stores.*

160g dark eating chocolate, chopped coarsely

160g unsalted butter, chopped

5 eggs, separated

¾ cup (165g) caster sugar

1 cup (125g) ground almonds

⅔ cup (50g) toasted flaked almonds, chopped coarsely

⅓ cup (35g) coarsely grated dark eating chocolate

1 cup (140g) caramelised almonds

DARK CHOCOLATE GANACHE

125g dark eating chocolate, chopped coarsely

⅓ cup (80ml) whipping cream

1  Preheat oven to 180°C/160°C fan-assisted. Grease deep 22cm-round cake tin; line the base and side with two layers of baking parchment.

2  Stir chopped chocolate and butter in small saucepan over low heat until smooth; cool to room temperature.

3  Beat egg yolks and sugar in small bowl with electric mixer until thick and creamy. Transfer to large bowl; fold in chocolate mixture, ground almonds, flaked almonds and grated chocolate.

4  Beat egg whites in small bowl with electric mixer until soft peaks form; fold into chocolate mixture, in two batches. Pour mixture into prepared tin; bake, uncovered, about 45 minutes. Stand cake in tin 15 minutes; turn cake, top-side up, onto wire rack to cool.

5  Meanwhile, make dark chocolate ganache.

6  Spread ganache over top of cake, decorate cake with caramelised almonds; stand 30 minutes before serving.

**DARK CHOCOLATE GANACHE** Stir chocolate and cream in small saucepan over low heat until smooth.

# Flourless chocolate hazelnut cake

**preparation time** 20 minutes (plus cooling time) **cooking time** 1 hour **serves** 8

⅓ cup (35g) cocoa powder

⅓ cup (80ml) hot water

150g dark eating chocolate, melted

150g butter, melted

1⅓ cups (295g) firmly packed brown sugar

1 cup (100g) ground hazelnuts (see tip)

4 eggs, separated

1 tablespoon cocoa powder, extra

1  Preheat oven to 180°C/160°C fan-assisted. Grease deep 20cm-round cake tin; line base and side with baking parchment.

2  Blend cocoa with the water in large bowl until smooth. Stir in chocolate, butter, sugar, ground hazelnuts and egg yolks.

3  Beat egg whites in small bowl with electric mixer until soft peaks form; fold into chocolate mixture in two batches.

4  Pour mixture into prepared tin; bake, uncovered, about 1 hour. Stand cake in tin 15 minutes; turn onto wire rack, top-side up, to cool. Dust with sifted extra cocoa.

**tips** Our flourless cake confirms that marrying hazelnuts and chocolate in a recipe is a match made in heaven. If you wish, you can roast, skin and process whole hazelnuts to make the ground hazelnuts.
Similarly, you can dot the top of the finished cake with whole roasted nuts before you serve it, either warm or at room temperature.

# Black forest gateau

250g butter

1 tablespoon instant coffee powder

1½ cups (375ml) hot water

200g dark eating chocolate, chopped

2 cups (440g) caster sugar

1½ cups (225g) self-raising flour

1 cup (150g) plain flour

¼ cup (25g) cocoa powder

2 eggs

2 teaspoons vanilla essence

600ml whipping cream

¼ cup (60ml) kirsch

2 x 425g cans black cherries, drained, pitted

1 Preheat oven to 150°C/130°C fan-assisted. Grease deep 23cm-round cake tin, line base and side with baking parchment; grease parchment well.

2 Melt butter in medium saucepan, stir in combined coffee and hot water, then chocolate and sugar; stir over low heat, without boiling, until smooth. Transfer to large bowl, cool until warm. Beat mixture on low speed with electric mixer; gradually beat in sifted dry ingredients, in three batches. Beat in eggs, one at a time, then essence. Pour into prepared tin. Bake cake about 1¾ hours. Stand in tin 5 minutes before turning onto wire rack to cool.

3 Beat cream until firm peaks form. Trim top of cake to make it flat. Split cake into three layers. Place one layer on serving plate, brush with one-third of the kirsch, top with one-third of the cream and half of the cherries. Repeat layering once more, then top with cake-top. Brush top of cake with remaining kirsch; spread with remaining cream.

tips Gateau will keep for up to 3 days, covered, in the refrigerator. Decorate the gateau with fresh cherries and chocolate shavings, if desired.

cakes

# Mississippi mud cake

**preparation time** 25 minutes (plus cooling time)  **cooking time** 1 hour 35 minutes  **serves** 10

*This popular cake is a delectable alternative to fruit cake for weddings and other occasions. It is also wonderful after dinner with coffee, served warm or at room temperature with double cream.*

250g butter, chopped

150g dark eating chocolate, chopped

2 cups (440g) caster sugar

1 cup (250ml) hot water

⅓ cup (80ml) coffee-flavoured liqueur

1 tablespoon instant coffee powder

1½ cups (225g) plain flour

¼ cup (35g) self-raising flour

¼ cup (25g) cocoa powder

2 eggs, beaten lightly

1 Preheat oven to 170°C/150°C fan-assisted. Grease deep 20cm-round cake tin; line base and side with baking parchment.

2 Combine butter, chocolate, sugar, the water, liqueur and coffee powder in medium saucepan. Using wooden spoon, stir over low heat until chocolate melts.

3 Transfer mixture to large bowl; cool 15 minutes. Whisk in combined sifted flours and cocoa powder, then egg. Pour mixture into prepared tin.

4 Bake cake about 1½ hours. Stand cake in tin 30 minutes before turning onto wire rack; turn cake top-side up to cool.

**tips**  Cover the cake loosely with foil about halfway through the baking time if it starts to overbrown.
The cake will keep for up to one week in an airtight container in refrigerator.

# Rich truffle mud cake

**preparation time** 15 minutes (plus cooling and refrigeration time)  **cooking time** 1 hour  **serves** 12 to 14

*This very rich cake is perfect for the grand finale to a dinner party, and should be made a day ahead and served cold. The cake is almost like a huge truffle in texture; note that no flour is used in the recipe.*

6 eggs

½ cup (110g) firmly packed brown sugar

400g dark eating chocolate, melted

1 cup (250ml) double cream

⅓ cup (80ml) cointreau

1 Preheat oven to 180°C/160°C fan-assisted. Grease deep 22cm-round cake tin; line base and side with baking parchment.

2 Beat eggs and sugar in large bowl with electric mixer about 5 minutes or until thick and creamy. With motor operating, gradually beat in barely warm chocolate; beat until combined.

3 Using metal spoon, gently fold in combined cream and liqueur. Pour mixture into prepared tin. Place tin in baking dish; pour enough boiling water into dish to come halfway up side of tin.

4 Bake cake 30 minutes. Cover loosely with foil; bake further 30 minutes. Discard foil; cool cake in tin.

5 Turn cake onto serving plate, cover; refrigerate overnight. Serve dusted with a little sifted cocoa powder, if desired.

**tips**  Any liqueur can be substituted for the citrus-flavoured cointreau, if you prefer; try rum or frangelico.
Cake will keep for up to four days in an airtight container in the refrigerator.
This cake is delicious served with raspberries and raspberry coulis.

# Chocolate mocha dacquoise terrine

**preparation time** 20 minutes (plus cooling and refrigeration time)  **cooking time** 45 minutes  **serves** 12

*A classic dacquoise is a layered meringue sandwiched with a butter-cream filling. It is served cold, often with a complementary seasonal fruit, or sometimes with nuts mixed into the buttercream.*

4 egg whites

1 cup (220g) caster sugar

2 tablespoons cocoa powder

200g dark eating chocolate, chopped coarsely

¾ cup (180ml) double cream

2 teaspoons cocoa powder, extra

MOCHA BUTTERCREAM

1 tablespoon instant coffee powder

2 tablespoons boiling water

100g unsalted butter, softened

2¼ cups (360g) icing sugar

1 Preheat oven to 150°C/130°C fan-assisted. Line each of three oven trays with baking parchment; draw a 10cm x 25cm rectangle on each baking-parchment-lined tray.

2 Beat egg whites in medium bowl with electric mixer until soft peaks form. Gradually add sugar, beating after each addition until sugar dissolves; fold in sifted cocoa.

3 Spread meringue mixture evenly over drawn rectangles; bake, uncovered, about 45 minutes or until meringue is dry. Turn off oven; cool meringues in oven with door ajar.

4 Meanwhile, stir chocolate and cream in small saucepan over low heat until smooth, transfer to small bowl; refrigerate until firm. Beat chocolate mixture with electric mixer about 20 seconds or until just changed in colour.

5 Make mocha buttercream.

6 Place one meringue layer on serving plate; spread with half of the chocolate mixture, then top with half of the buttercream. Top with another meringue layer; spread with remaining chocolate mixture, then with remaining buttercream. Top with last meringue layer, cover; refrigerate 3 hours or overnight. To serve, dust with sifted extra cocoa powder.

MOCHA BUTTERCREAM Dissolve coffee powder with the boiling water in small bowl; cool 10 minutes. Beat butter in small bowl with electric mixer until pale in colour; gradually add icing sugar, beating until combined. Beat in coffee mixture.

# Rich chocolate fruit cakes

**preparation time** 40 minutes (plus standing and cooling time)  **cooking time** 1 hour 45 minutes  **makes** 8

1 cup (170g) pitted prunes

1 cup (140g) pitted dried dates

1 cup (150g) raisins

½ cup (75g) muscatels (see tip)

1 cup (200g) dried figs

5 (100g) glacé orange slices

1½ cups (375ml) Irish whiskey

1½ cups (330g) firmly packed dark brown sugar

185g butter, softened

3 eggs

½ cup (50g) ground hazelnuts

1½ cups (225g) plain flour

2 tablespoons cocoa powder

1 teaspoon mixed spice

½ teaspoon ground nutmeg

½ teaspoon bicarbonate of soda

150g dark eating chocolate, chopped finely

¼ cup (60ml) water

2 tablespoons cocoa powder, extra

1 cup (150g) muscatels, extra

1 Chop all fruit finely. Combine fruit and ¾ cup of the whiskey in large bowl, cover with cling film; stand overnight.

2 Preheat oven to 120°C/100°C fan-assisted. Line eight deep 8cm-round cake tins with two thicknesses of baking parchment, extending paper 5cm above sides of tins.

3 Stir remaining whiskey and ¾ cup of the sugar in small saucepan over heat until sugar dissolves; bring to the boil. Remove from heat; cool syrup 20 minutes.

4 Meanwhile, beat butter and remaining sugar in small bowl with electric mixer until combined; beat in eggs, one at a time. Add butter mixture to fruit mixture; mix well. Mix in ground hazelnuts, sifted dry ingredients, chocolate and ½ cup of the cooled syrup. Spread mixture into tins.

5 Bake cakes about 1¾ hours.

6 Bring remaining syrup and the water to the boil in small saucepan; boil for 3 minutes or until thickened slightly. Brush hot cakes with half of the hot syrup, cover cakes with foil; cool in tins.

7 Divide reserved muscatels into eight small bunches; place bunches in remaining syrup. Stand in syrup until cool, drain.

8 Dust cakes with extra sifted cocoa, top with muscatel bunches.

**tip** Muscatels are large dried grapes on the stem, available from gourmet food stores and some health food stores. Buy 200g muscatels for these cakes, use one-third in the cake mixture and the rest for decorating.

# Apricot chocolate chip cake

**preparation time** 30 minutes (plus standing time)  **cooking time** 1 hour 15 minutes (plus cooling time)  **serves** 8

1 cup (150g) chopped dried apricots

1 cup (250ml) apricot nectar (see tip)

125g butter, softened

⅔ cup (150g) raw sugar

2 eggs, separated

1½ cups (120g) desiccated coconut

1½ cups (225g) self-raising flour

½ cup (95g) dark chocolate chips

1 Preheat oven to 180°C/160°C fan-assisted. Grease deep 20cm-round cake tin; line base with baking parchment.

2 Combine apricots and nectar in medium bowl; stand 1 hour.

3 Beat butter and sugar in small bowl with electric mixer until light and fluffy. Add egg yolks, beat until combined.

4 Transfer mixture to large bowl, stir in coconut then half the sifted flour and half the apricot mixture. Stir in remaining flour, remaining apricot mixture then chocolate chips.

5 Beat egg whites in small bowl with electric mixer until soft peaks form; fold into apricot mixture.

6 Spread mixture into tin; bake about 1¼ hours. Stand cake 5 minutes before turning onto wire rack to cool.

7 Serve cake dusted with sifted icing sugar, if desired.

**tips** Apricot nectar is a sweetened purée of apricots, available in cans or bottles. If you can't get hold of it, buy a can of apricots in syrup and pass them through a sieve to obtain a thick purée. Cake will keep in an airtight container for up to three days.


# Chocolate panettone

**preparation time** 40 minutes (plus standing time)  **cooking time** 25 minutes (plus cooling time)  **makes** 6

¾ cup (180ml) warm milk

1 teaspoon caster sugar

2 x 7g sachets (1 tablespoon) dried yeast

2¼ cups (335g) plain flour

⅓ cup (35g) cocoa powder

¼ cup (55g) caster sugar, extra

1 teaspoon coarse cooking salt

1 teaspoon vanilla extract

50g butter, softened

2 eggs

2 egg yolks

½ cup (90g) raisins

⅓ cup (45g) coarsely chopped pitted dried dates

½ cup (95g) dark chocolate chips

1 egg, extra

2 teaspoons icing sugar

1 Combine milk, caster sugar and yeast in medium jug. Cover; stand in warm place about 10 minutes or until frothy.

2 Sift flour, cocoa, extra caster sugar and salt into large bowl; stir in yeast mixture, extract, butter, eggs, yolks, fruit and chocolate chips. Knead dough on floured surface about 10 minutes or until elastic. Place dough in greased large bowl. Cover; stand in warm place about 1 hour or until doubled in size.

3 Preheat oven to 200°C/180°C fan-assisted. Line 6-hole large (¾-cup/180ml) muffin pan with paper cases. To make your own paper cases, cut six 15cm squares from baking parchment. Cut six 15cm squares from standard photocopier paper. Line pan first with paper, then with baking parchment set at a different angle.

4 Knead dough on floured surface about 10 minutes or until dough loses its stickiness. Divide dough into six equal portions and press into pan holes. Cover loosely, stand in warm place about 30 minutes or until doubled in size. Brush panettone with extra egg.

5 Bake panettone 25 minutes. Stand in pan 5 minutes; turn top-side up, onto wire rack to cool. Dust with sifted icing sugar.

# Chocolate drambuie fruit cake

**preparation time** 50 minutes (plus standing time)  **cooking time** 4 hours 30 minutes (plus cooling time)  **serves** 36

2⅓ cups (375g) sultanas

2¼ cups (375g) raisins, chopped coarsely

1⅔ cups (230g) currants

1½ cups (250g) prunes, pitted, chopped coarsely

1½ cups (210g) dried dates, pitted, chopped coarsely

¾ cup (120g) mixed peel

⅔ cup (140g) red glacé cherries, quartered

1⅓ cups (330ml) Drambuie

⅓ cup (115g) honey

1 tablespoon finely grated lemon rind

250g butter, softened

1½ cups (330g) firmly packed dark brown sugar

6 eggs

90g dark eating chocolate, grated

1¼ cups (150g) pecans, chopped

2 cups (300g) plain flour

1 cup (150g) self-raising flour

¼ cup (25g) cocoa powder

1  Combine fruit, 1 cup (250ml) of the Drambuie, honey and rind in large bowl. Cover tightly with cling film; store in a cool, dark place overnight or up to a week, stirring every day.

2  On the day of baking, preheat oven to 120°C/100°C fan-assisted. Grease six-hole large (¾-cup/180ml) muffin pan. Grease deep 22cm-round or deep 19cm-square cake tin; line base and side(s) with four thicknesses of baking parchment, extending paper 5cm above edge(s).

3  Beat butter and sugar in medium bowl with electric mixer until just combined. Add eggs, one at a time, beating until combined between additions. Stir into fruit mixture with chocolate and nuts. Stir in sifted dry ingredients, in two batches.

4  Fill each hole of muffin pan, level to the top, with mixture; spread remaining mixture into cake tin. Decorate tops with extra pecans and glacé cherries, if desired.

5  Bake muffins 1½ hours (cake can stand while muffins are baking). Brush hot muffins with some of the remaining Drambuie; cover with foil, cool in pan.

6  Increase oven temperature to 150°C/130°C fan-assisted. Bake large cake 3 hours. Brush hot cake with remaining Drambuie; cover hot cake with foil; cool in tin overnight.

**tips**  You can make a larger cake by using a deep 25cm-round or deep 23cm-square cake tin, if you prefer; allow about 4 to 4½ hours for baking.

Cake can be made up to three months ahead; store in an airtight container in the refrigerator, or freeze for up to 12 months.

# Biscuits & slices

## Chewy choc-chunk cookies

**preparation time** 25 minutes (plus chilling time)  **cooking time** 10 minutes per tray (plus cooling time)  **makes** 20

2 eggs

1⅓ cups (295g) firmly packed brown sugar

1 teaspoon vanilla extract

1 cup (150g) plain flour

¾ cup (110g) self-raising flour

½ teaspoon bicarbonate of soda

½ cup (125ml) vegetable oil

1 cup (120g) coarsely chopped toasted pecans

¾ cup (120g) coarsely chopped raisins

1 cup (150g) dark eating chocolate, chopped coarsely

½ cup (95g) white chocolate chips

1  Preheat oven to 200°C/180°C fan-assisted). Grease oven trays.

2  Beat eggs, sugar and extract in small bowl with electric mixer about 1 minute or until mixture becomes lighter in colour.

3  Stir in sifted dry ingredients then remaining ingredients (the mixture will be soft). Cover bowl; refrigerate 1 hour.

4  Roll heaped tablespoons of the mixture into balls; place onto trays about 6cm apart, flatten into 6cm rounds.

5  Bake about 10 minutes or until browned lightly. Stand cookies on trays 5 minutes; transfer to wire rack to cool.

**tips**  Cookies can be made up to one week ahead; keep in an airtight container.
Walnuts can be substituted for pecans, if desired.

# Chocolate melting moments

**preparation time** 15 minutes (plus cooling time) **cooking time** 10 minutes **makes** 28

125g butter, chopped

2 tablespoons icing sugar

¾ cup (110g) plain flour

2 tablespoons cornflour

2 tablespoons cocoa powder

¼ cup (85g) chocolate hazelnut spread

1 Preheat oven to 180°C/160°C fan-assisted. Lightly grease two oven trays.

2 Beat butter and sugar in small bowl with electric mixer until light and fluffy. Stir in sifted dry ingredients, in two batches.

3 Spoon mixture into piping bag fitted with 5mm fluted tube. Pipe directly onto prepared trays, allowing 3cm between each biscuit; bake about 10 minutes or until biscuits are firm. Stand biscuits 5 minutes; transfer to wire rack to cool. Sandwich biscuits with spread to serve.

**tip** Strawberry or raspberry jam can also be used instead of chocolate hazelnut spread.

# Choc-hazelnut cookie sandwiches

**preparation time** 25 minutes (plus refrigeration time) **cooking time** 10 minutes **makes** 30

80g butter, chopped

1 teaspoon vanilla extract

¼ cup (55g) caster sugar

1 egg

½ cup (50g) ground hazelnuts

¾ cup (110g) plain flour

¼ cup (25g) cocoa powder

1 tablespoon cocoa powder, extra

CHOC-HAZELNUT CREAM

100g dark eating chocolate, melted

50g butter, softened

⅓ cup (110g) chocolate hazelnut spread

1 Beat butter, extract, sugar and egg in small bowl with electric mixer until light and fluffy; stir in ground hazelnuts with sifted flour and cocoa. Wrap dough in cling film; refrigerate about 1 hour or until firm.

2 Preheat oven to 180°C/160°C fan-assisted. Lightly grease two oven trays.

3 Roll dough between two sheets of baking parchment until 3mm thick. Using 4cm-fluted cutter, cut 60 rounds from dough. Place rounds on prepared trays; bake about 8 minutes. Stand biscuits 5 minutes; transfer onto wire rack to cool.

4 Make choc-hazelnut cream; spoon into piping bag fitted with large fluted tube. Pipe cream onto one biscuit; sandwich with another biscuit. Place on wire rack set over tray; repeat with remaining biscuits and cream. When all sandwiches are on rack, dust with extra sifted cocoa.

**CHOC-HAZELNUT CREAM** Beat cooled chocolate, butter and spread in small bowl with electric mixer until thick and glossy.

# Choc-chip cookies

**preparation time** 40 minutes (plus refrigeration time) **cooking time** 15 minutes **makes** 40

*Originally called toll house cookies, these biscuits were invented by the owner of the Toll House Inn, Ruth Graves Wakefield, in 1930s Massachusetts. She added bits of dark chocolate to her favourite cookie dough, expecting them to melt during baking. Instead, the chocolate held its shape and became delicate and creamy – and the classic choc-chip cookie was born!*

250g butter, softened

1 teaspoon vanilla extract

¾ cup (165g) caster sugar

¾ cup (165g) firmly packed brown sugar

1 egg

2¼ cups (335g) plain flour

1 teaspoon bicarbonate of soda

300g dark cooking chocolate, chopped finely

1 Preheat oven to 180°C/160°C fan-assisted.

2 Beat butter, extract, sugars and egg in small bowl with electric mixer until light and fluffy. Transfer to large bowl.

3 Stir combined sifted flour and bicarbonate of soda, in two batches, into egg mixture. Stir in chocolate, cover; refrigerate 1 hour.

4 Roll level tablespoons of the dough into balls; place on greased oven trays 3cm apart. Bake, uncovered, about 12 minutes. Cool cookies on trays.

# Triple-choc cookies

**preparation time** 10 minutes **cooking time** 10 minutes **makes** 36

125g butter, chopped

½ teaspoon vanilla extract

1¼ cups (250g) firmly packed brown sugar

1 egg

1 cup (150g) plain flour

¼ cup (35g) self-raising flour

1 teaspoon bicarbonate of soda

⅓ cup (35g) cocoa powder

½ cup (85g) chopped raisins

½ cup (95g) milk chocolate chips

100g white eating chocolate, chopped coarsely

100g dark eating chocolate, chopped coarsely

1 Preheat oven to 180°C/160°C fan-assisted. Lightly grease two oven trays.

2 Beat butter, extract, sugar and egg in small bowl with electric mixer until smooth; do not overbeat. Stir in sifted dry ingredients, then raisins, chocolate chips and white and dark chocolate.

3 Drop level tablespoons of mixture onto prepared trays, allowing 5cm between each cookie; bake about 10 minutes. Stand cookies 5 minutes; transfer to wire rack to cool.

tips  For a firmer cookie, bake an extra 2 minutes.
Serve these cookies with hot chocolate for a late-night treat.

biscuits & slices

# Fudgy-wudgy chocolate cookies

**preparation time** 10 minutes  **cooking time** 10 minutes  **makes** 24

125g butter, chopped

1 teaspoon vanilla extract

1¼ cups (250g) firmly packed brown sugar

1 egg

1 cup (150g) plain flour

¼ cup (35g) self-raising flour

1 teaspoon bicarbonate of soda

⅓ cup (35g) cocoa powder

½ cup (85g) raisins

¾ cup (100g) toasted macadamia nuts, chopped coarsely

½ cup (95g) dark chocolate chips

100g dark cooking chocolate, chopped coarsely

1 Preheat oven to 180°C/160°C fan-assisted. Line three oven trays with baking parchment.

2 Beat butter, extract, sugar and egg in medium bowl with electric mixer until smooth. Stir in combined sifted flours, soda and cocoa; stir in raisins, nuts, chocolate chips and dark chocolate.

3 Drop rounded tablespoons of mixture onto prepared trays about 4cm apart; press each with fork to flatten slightly. Bake 10 minutes. Stand 5 minutes; transfer cookies to wire rack to cool.

**tips** Cookies can be made up to four days ahead; store in an airtight container.
Other nuts, such as walnuts or pecans, can be used instead of macadamias.

# Florentines

**preparation time** 25 minutes  **cooking time** 35 minutes  **makes** 20

30g butter

2 tablespoons brown sugar

1 tablespoon golden syrup

¼ teaspoon ground ginger

2 tablespoons plain flour

1 tablespoon finely chopped glacé apricots

1 tablespoon finely chopped glacé cherries

¼ cup (20g) flaked almonds

75g dark eating chocolate, melted

1 Preheat oven to 180°C/160°C fan-assisted. Combine butter, sugar and syrup in a pan. Stir over low heat until sugar dissolves. Bring to boil. Using a sugar thermometer, bring mixture to 114°C, or, when a small amount is dropped into cold water and can then be rolled into a soft ball.

2 Remove from heat, stir in ginger, flour, apricots, cherries and almonds. Drop level teaspoons of mixture on a greased oven tray, leaving 6cm between each. Cook six florentines at a time.

3 Bake about 7 minutes or until browned. Neaten edges while hot; stand florentines for 1 minute; transfer to a wire rack to cool.

4 Spread cooled chocolate thinly over flat side of each florentine; run a fork through chocolate in a wavy pattern. Stand chocolate-side-up until set.

**tip** Florentines can be made a day ahead. Store in an airtight container in a cool, dry place.

biscuits & slices

44

# Mocha cookies

preparation time 20 minutes  cooking time 12 minutes  MAKES 20

150g butter, softened

¾ cup (165g) firmly packed brown sugar

1 egg yolk

2 teaspoons instant coffee granules

1 tablespoon hot water

1½ cups (225g) plain flour

1 tablespoon cocoa powder

20 large chocolate buttons

1 Preheat oven to 180°C/160°C fan-assisted. Grease and line two oven trays with baking parchment.

2 Beat butter, sugar, egg yolk and combined coffee and water in small bowl with electric mixer until smooth. Transfer mixture to large bowl; stir in sifted flour and cocoa, in two batches. Knead dough on floured surface until smooth.

3 Roll level tablespoons of mixture into balls; place 5cm apart on trays, flatten slightly. Press one chocolate button into centre of each cookie; bake about 12 minutes. Cool cookies on trays.

# Choc-nut biscotti

preparation time 35 minutes (plus cooling time)  cooking time 50 minutes  makes 60

1 cup (220g) caster sugar

2 eggs

1⅔ cups (250g) plain flour

1 teaspoon baking powder

1 cup (150g) toasted shelled pistachios

½ cup (70g) slivered almonds

¼ cup (25g) cocoa powder

1 Preheat oven to 180°C/160°C fan-assisted.

2 Whisk sugar and eggs in medium bowl. Stir in sifted flour, baking powder and nuts; mix to a sticky dough.

3 Knead dough on lightly floured surface until smooth. Divide dough into two portions. Using floured hands, knead one portion on lightly floured surface until smooth, but still slightly sticky; divide into four pieces. Roll each piece into 25cm log shape. Knead remaining portion with cocoa until smooth, divide into two pieces. Roll each piece of chocolate mixture into 25cm log shape.

4 Place one chocolate log on lightly greased oven tray. Place a plain log on each side, press gently together. Repeat with remaining logs.

5 Bake about 30 minutes or until browned lightly. Cool on tray 10 minutes. Reduce oven to 150°C/130°C fan-assisted.

6 Using a serrated knife, cut logs diagonally into 5mm slices. Place slices, in single layer, on ungreased oven trays.

7 Bake about 20 minutes or until dry and crisp, turning halfway through cooking; cool on wire racks.

biscuits & slices

# Mocha hazelnut biscotti

**preparation time** 20 minutes (plus cooling time)  **cooking time** 50 minutes  **makes** 50

1¼ cups (185g) hazelnuts

3 eggs

½ cup (100g) firmly packed brown sugar

½ cup (110g) caster sugar

1½ cups (225g) plain flour

1 cup (150g) self-raising flour

⅓ cup (35g) cocoa powder

2 teaspoons instant coffee powder

2 tablespoons frangelico liqueur

100g dark eating chocolate, grated finely

1 Preheat oven to 180°C/160°C fan-assisted. Spread nuts in single layer on oven tray; bake about 5 minutes or until the skins begin to split. Rub nuts firmly in clean tea towel to remove skins.

2 Beat eggs and sugars in medium bowl with electric mixer until smooth and changed in colour. Stir in sifted flours and cocoa, combined coffee and liqueur, chocolate and nuts; mix to a firm dough.

3 Gently knead dough on floured surface until smooth; divide dough in half. Shape each half into a 7cm x 20cm log. Place logs on greased large oven tray. Bake, uncovered, about 30 minutes or until firm. Cool on tray 15 minutes.

4 Using a serrated knife, cut logs diagonally into 5mm slices; place slices, in single layer, on ungreased oven trays. Bake biscotti further 15 minutes or until both sides are dry and crisp; cool. Serve with coffee, if desired.

**tip** This recipe can be made two weeks ahead. Suitable to freeze.

# Chocolate peanut drizzles

**preparation time** 15 minutes (plus standing time)  **cooking time** 30 minutes  **makes** 25

395g can sweetened condensed milk

½ cup (140g) crunchy peanut butter

3 cups (120g) cornflakes

80g dark eating chocolate, melted

1 Preheat oven to 200°C/180°C fan-assisted.

2 Combine milk, peanut butter and cornflakes in large bowl. Drop level tablespoons of mixture, 5cm apart, onto two oven trays. Bake about 12 minutes; cool on trays.

3 Drizzle with melted chocolate; stand at room temperature until chocolate sets.

# Triple chocolate brownies

preparation time 15 minutes  cooking time 40 minutes  makes 18

125g butter, chopped

200g dark eating chocolate, chopped finely

¾ cup (165g) caster sugar

2 eggs, beaten lightly

1 cup (150g) plain flour

150g white eating chocolate, chopped

100g milk eating chocolate, chopped

cocoa powder or icing sugar, for dusting

1 Preheat oven to 180°C/160°C fan-assisted. Grease deep 19cm-square cake tin, line base and sides with baking parchment.
2 Combine butter and dark chocolate in large saucepan; stir over very low heat until melted. Remove from heat.
3 Stir in sugar, then eggs. Stir in sifted flour, then chopped chocolate. Spread mixture into prepared tin.
4 Bake about 35 minutes or until brownie is firm to touch. Cool in tin.
5 Cut into squares. Serve dusted with sifted cocoa or icing sugar, if desired.

tip This recipe can be made 4 days ahead. Suitable to freeze.

# Chocolate & peanut butter swirl

preparation time 15 minutes (plus standing time)  cooking time 10 minutes  makes about 72

360g white eating chocolate, chopped coarsely

½ cup (140g) smooth peanut butter

400g dark eating chocolate, chopped coarsely

1 Grease 20cm x 30cm baking tin; line base and sides with baking parchment, extending 5cm above long edges of tin.
2 Stir white chocolate in small heatproof bowl over simmering water until smooth; cool 5 minutes. Add peanut butter; stir until smooth.
3 Stir dark chocolate in small heatproof bowl over simmering water until smooth; cool slightly.
4 Drop alternate spoonfuls of white chocolate mixture and dark chocolate into prepared tin. Gently shake tin to level mixture; pull a skewer backwards and forwards through mixture several times for a marbled effect. Stand at room temperature about 2 hours or until set; cut into small pieces.

tip Chocolate suitable to melt in microwave oven; heat on medium (55%) about 1 minute, pausing to stir twice.

# Chocolate panforte

**preparation time** 25 minutes (plus standing time)  **cooking time** 55 minutes  **makes** 30

2 sheets rice paper

¾ cup (110g) plain flour

2 tablespoons cocoa powder

½ teaspoon ground cinnamon

½ teaspoon ground ginger

½ cup (150g) coarsely chopped glacé figs

½ cup (85g) dried dates, pitted, halved

½ cup (125g) coarsely chopped glacé peaches

¼ cup (50g) red glacé cherries, halved

¼ cup (50g) green glacé cherries, halved

½ cup (80g) toasted blanched almonds

½ cup (75g) toasted unsalted cashews

½ cup (75g) toasted hazelnuts

½ cup (75g) toasted macadamia nuts

⅓ cup (120g) honey

⅓ cup (75g) caster sugar

⅓ cup (75g) firmly packed brown sugar

2 tablespoons water

100g dark eating chocolate, melted

1   Preheat oven to 170°C/150°C fan-assisted. Grease 20cm sandwich tin; line base with rice paper sheets.

2   Sift flour, cocoa and spices into large bowl; stir in fruit and nuts.

3   Combine honey, sugars and the water in small saucepan; stir over heat, without boiling, until sugar dissolves. Simmer; uncovered, without stirring, 5 minutes. Pour hot syrup, then chocolate, into nut mixture; stir until well combined. Press mixture firmly into prepared tin.

4   Bake about 45 minutes; cool in tin.

5   Remove panforte from tin; wrap in foil. Stand overnight; cut into thin wedges to serve.

**tip**  Rice paper can be found in specialist-food stores and some supermarkets and delicatessens.

# No-bowl choc-chip slice

**preparation time** 10 minutes (plus cooling time)  **cooking time** 30 minutes  **makes** about 18

90g butter, melted

1 cup (100g) digestive biscuit crumbs

1½ cups (285g) dark chocolate chips

1 cup (70g) shredded coconut

1 cup (140g) crushed mixed nuts

395g can sweetened condensed milk

1   Preheat oven to 180°C/160°C fan-assisted. Grease 23cm-square baking tin; line base and sides with baking parchment.

2   Pour butter into prepared tin; sprinkle evenly with biscuit crumbs, chocolate chips, coconut and nuts. Drizzle with condensed milk.

3   Bake about 30 minutes. Cool in tin; cut into slices.

# Chocolate macadamia slice

preparation time 15 minutes (plus refrigeration time) cooking time 5 minutes makes 30

200g butter, chopped

⅓ cup (115g) golden syrup

⅓ cup (35g) drinking chocolate

¼ cup (25g) cocoa powder

500g plain sweet biscuits, chopped finely

½ cup (75g) toasted macadamias, chopped coarsely

200g dark eating chocolate

1  Line 20cm x 30cm baking tin with cling film.
2  Combine butter, syrup, drinking chocolate and sifted cocoa in medium saucepan; stir over medium heat until mixture is smooth. Add biscuits and nuts; stir to combine.
3  Press mixture into prepared tin, cover; refrigerate until firm.
4  Stir chocolate in medium heatproof bowl over simmering water until smooth. Spread chocolate over slice; refrigerate, uncovered, until firm. Cut into pieces to serve.

tip  Macadamias can be replaced with any other variety of nut.


# Hazelnut caramel slice

preparation time 15 minutes (plus refrigeration time) cooking time 35 minutes makes about 20

200g butter, chopped

½ cup (50g) cocoa powder

2 cups (440g) firmly packed brown sugar

1 teaspoon vanilla extract

2 eggs, beaten lightly

1½ cups (225g) plain flour

200g dark eating chocolate, melted, cooled

1 tablespoon vegetable oil

CARAMEL FILLING

180g butter, chopped

½ cup (110g) caster sugar

2 tablespoons golden syrup

¾ cup (180ml) sweetened condensed milk

1¼ cups (175g) toasted hazelnuts

1  Preheat oven to 170°C/150°C fan-assisted. Grease 20cm x 30cm baking tin; line base and two long sides with baking parchment.
2  Combine butter and cocoa in medium saucepan; stir over low heat until smooth. Add sugar; stir until dissolved. Remove from heat; add extract, egg and sifted flour, mix well. Spread mixture into prepared tin, bake 20 minutes; cool.
3  Make caramel filling. Quickly spread filling evenly over base; refrigerate at least 30 minutes or until firm. Combine chocolate and oil in small bowl, spread over caramel filling; refrigerate until set. Cut into pieces to serve.
   CARAMEL FILLING  Combine butter, sugar, syrup and condensed milk in medium saucepan; stir over low heat until butter is melted. Increase heat to medium and simmer, stirring, about 10 minutes or until mixture is dark caramel in colour. Remove from heat; stir in hazelnuts.

tip  Slice can be made 2 days ahead and kept, covered, in refrigerator.

# Chocolate rum & raisin slice

**preparation time** 10 minutes (plus cooling time) **cooking time** 35 minutes **makes** about 15

125g butter, chopped

200g dark eating chocolate, chopped

½ cup (110g) caster sugar

1 cup (170g) coarsely chopped raisins

2 eggs, beaten lightly

1½ cups (225g) plain flour

1 tablespoon dark rum

1 Preheat oven to 170°C/150°C fan-assisted. Grease 19cm x 29cm baking tin.

2 Combine butter, chocolate, sugar and raisins in medium saucepan; stir over low heat until chocolate is melted. Cool to room temperature. Stir in remaining ingredients, mix well; spread mixture into prepared tin.

3 Bake about 30 minutes or until just firm; cool in tin. Serve dusted with sifted icing sugar, if desired.

**tip** This slice can be made a week ahead; store in an airtight container.

# Nanaimo bars

**preparation time** 10 minutes (plus cooling time) **cooking time** 35 minutes **makes** about 15

185g butter, chopped

100g dark eating chocolate, coarsely chopped

1 egg

2 cups (200g) digestive biscuit crumbs

1 cup (80g) desiccated coconut

⅔ cup (80g) finely chopped pecans

FILLING

60g butter, softened

1 teaspoon vanilla extract

2 cups (320g) icing sugar

2 tablespoons custard powder

¼ cup (60ml) milk

TOPPING

30g dark eating chocolate

15g butter

1 Grease 19cm x 29cm rectangular baking tin; line base and two long sides with baking parchment, extending paper 2cm above edges.

2 Make filling.

3 Melt butter and chocolate in large bowl over hot water until smooth; stir in egg.

4 Add biscuit crumbs, coconut and nuts; mix well. Press mixture firmly over base of tin. Spread evenly with filling. Refrigerate until firm.

5 Make topping.

6 Drizzle slice with topping; refrigerate 3 hours or overnight until set. Cut into pieces before serving.

**FILLING** Beat butter and extract in small bowl with electric mixer until as white as possible; gradually beat in sifted icing sugar and custard powder, then milk.

**TOPPING** Melt chocolate and butter in small bowl over hot water.

**tips** Nanaimo bars can be made up to two weeks ahead; keep, covered, in refrigerator.
The butter and chocolate for the base and topping can be melted together in a microwave oven.

# No-bake chocolate slice

**preparation time** 15 minutes (plus refrigeration time) **cooking time** 5 minutes **makes** 24

200g white marshmallows

1 tablespoon water

90g butter, chopped

200g dark eating chocolate, chopped coarsely

125g plain sweet biscuits, chopped coarsely

½ cup (125g) halved glacé cherries

½ cup (75g) toasted hazelnuts

½ cup (50g) walnuts

200g dark eating chocolate, melted, extra

60g butter, melted, extra

1 Grease two 8cm x 25cm baking tins; line bases and sides with baking parchment, extending 2cm above long edges of tins.

2 Combine marshmallows, the water and butter in medium saucepan. Stir constantly over low heat until marshmallows are melted. Remove pan from heat. Add chocolate; stir until melted.

3 Add biscuits, cherries and nuts to marshmallow mixture; stir gently until ingredients are combined. Spread mixture evenly into prepared tins (do not crush biscuits). Cover; refrigerate 1 hour.

4 Combine extra chocolate and extra butter; spread mixture evenly over slices. Refrigerate 1 hour or until firm. Remove slices from tins. Peel away paper; cut each into 12 pieces.

**tips** Slice can be made a week ahead and kept, covered, in refrigerator.
Pecans can be used instead of walnuts, if preferred.

# Chocolate nut slice

**preparation time** 15 minutes (plus refrigeration time) **cooking time** 5 minutes **makes** 24

½ x 395g can sweetened condensed milk

250g dark eating chocolate, melted

½ cup (70g) coarsely chopped roasted hazelnuts

½ cup (60g) coarsely chopped roasted pecans

½ cup (80g) coarsely chopped roasted blanched almonds

1 Grease 8cm x 26cm baking tin; line base and sides with baking parchment, extending paper 5cm above long sides.

2 Combine ingredients in medium bowl. Spread mixture into tin.

3 Refrigerate several hours or overnight until firm.

**tips** Any combination of nuts can be used.
Slice can be kept, wrapped in cling film and refrigerated, for up to four weeks..

# Pastries & tarts

## Chocolate almond tart

**preparation time** 35 minutes (plus freezing time)  **cooking time** 35 minutes  **serves** 4

50g dark eating chocolate, chopped coarsely

¼ cup (55g) caster sugar

1 tablespoon cocoa powder

½ cup (60g) ground almonds

20g cold unsalted butter, chopped finely

2 eggs

2 teaspoons brandy

2 sheets ready-rolled puff pastry

1  Process chocolate, sugar, cocoa and ground almonds in food processor until chocolate is chopped finely. Add butter and process until mixture begins to come together.

2  Add 1 egg and brandy; process to combine.

3  Cut one pastry sheet into 12cm x 24cm rectangle; cut the other into 14cm x 24cm rectangle. Leaving a 2cm border along all sides, cut even slits in centre of larger pastry sheet at 1.5cm intervals. Place smaller sheet on greased oven tray; spread centre with chocolate mixture, leaving a 2cm border. Brush edges with a little of the remaining beaten egg.

4  Top with other pastry sheet, press edges together. Freeze 10 minutes.

5  Preheat oven to 200°C/180°C fan-assisted.

6  Brush pastry lightly with remaining beaten egg. Bake about 35 minutes or until golden.

**tips**  This tart can be made 8 hours ahead. Suitable to freeze.

# Chocolate hazelnut croissants

preparation time 15 minutes  cooking time 15 minutes  makes 8

2 sheets ready-rolled puff pastry

⅓ cup (110g) chocolate hazelnut spread

30g dark eating chocolate, grated finely

25g butter, melted

1 tablespoon icing sugar

1 Preheat oven to 220°C/200°C fan-assisted. Lightly grease two oven trays.

2 Cut pastry sheets diagonally to make four triangles each. Spread chocolate hazelnut spread over triangles, leaving a 1cm border; sprinkle each evenly with grated chocolate.

3 Roll triangles, starting at wide end; place 3cm apart on prepared trays with the tips tucked under and the ends slightly curved in to form crescent shape. Brush croissants with melted butter.

4 Bake, uncovered, about 12 minutes or until croissants are browned lightly and cooked through. Dust croissants with icing sugar; serve warm or at room temperature.

# Chocolate butterscotch tartlets

preparation time 5 minutes (plus refrigeration time)  cooking time 10 minutes  makes 12

12 frozen tartlet cases

¼ cup (55g) firmly packed brown sugar

20g butter

¼ cup (60ml) double cream

150g dark eating chocolate, chopped coarsely

¼ cup (60ml) double cream, extra

2 tablespoons coarsely chopped toasted hazelnuts

1 tablespoon cocoa powder

1 Bake tartlet cases according to manufacturer's instructions.

2 Meanwhile, heat combined sugar, butter and cream in small saucepan, stirring until sugar dissolves. Reduce heat; simmer, uncovered, without stirring, 2 minutes. Cool 5 minutes. Stir in chocolate and extra cream; refrigerate 10 minutes.

3 Divide mixture among tartlet cases, sprinkle with nuts and sifted cocoa.

# Gourmet chocolate tart

preparation time 40 minutes (plus refrigeration time)  cooking time 40 minutes  serves 8

2 eggs

2 egg yolks

¼ cup (55g) caster sugar

250g dark eating chocolate, melted

200g butter, melted

TART SHELL

1½ cups (240g) plain flour

½ cup (110g) caster sugar

140g cold butter, chopped

1 egg, beaten lightly

1  Make tart shell, baking in preheated oven as instructed below, then reducing oven temperature to 180°C/160°C fan-assisted.

2  Whisk eggs, egg yolks and sugar in medium heatproof bowl over simmering water about 15 minutes or until light and fluffy. Gently whisk chocolate and butter into egg mixture.

3  Pour mixture into shell. Bake, uncovered, about 10 minutes or until filling is set; cool 10 minutes. Refrigerate 1 hour. Serve dusted with cocoa powder, if desired.

TART SHELL  Blend or process flour, sugar and butter until crumbly; add egg, process until ingredients just come together. Knead dough on floured surface until smooth. Enclose in cling film; refrigerate 30 minutes. Grease 24cm-round loose-base flan tin. Roll dough between sheets of baking parchment until large enough to line prepared tin. Lift dough onto tin; press into side, trim edge, prick base all over with fork. Cover; refrigerate 30 minutes. Preheat oven to 200°C/180°C fan-assisted. Place tin on oven tray; cover dough with baking parchment, fill with dried beans or rice. Bake, uncovered, 10 minutes. Remove paper and beans carefully from tin; bake, uncovered, further 5 minutes or until tart shell browns lightly. Cool to room temperature.

# Rich chocolate coconut tart

**preparation time** 10 minutes (plus refrigeration time)  **cooking time** 40 minutes  **serves** 12

1 cup (90g) desiccated coconut

1 egg white, beaten lightly

¼ cup (55g) caster sugar

300ml double cream

300g dark eating chocolate, chopped finely

4 egg yolks

2 teaspoons coffee-flavoured liqueur

1 Preheat oven to 150°C/130°C fan-assisted. Grease 20cm non-stick springform cake tin.

2 Combine coconut, egg white and caster sugar. Press mixture evenly over base and 4cm up side of prepared tin. Bake, uncovered, about 40 minutes or until golden. Cool.

3 Heat cream until almost boiling. Add chocolate, stir until smooth; cool slightly. Whisk egg yolks and liqueur into chocolate; strain. Pour chocolate mixture into coconut shell. Refrigerate 6 hours or until set.

4 Cut into thin wedges to serve.

**tips** To make it easier to remove pan base from tart, place base in upside down before lining with biscuit.
This tart can be made up to 8 hours ahead.
The tart filling is suitable to microwave.

# Mini chocolate éclairs

**preparation time** 25 minutes  **cooking time** 25 minutes  **makes** 16

20g butter

¼ cup (60ml) water

¼ cup (35g) plain flour

1 egg

300ml whipping cream, whipped

100g dark eating chocolate, melted

1 Preheat oven to 220°C/200°C fan-assisted. Grease two oven trays.

2 Combine butter with the water in small saucepan; bring to the boil. Add flour; beat with wooden spoon over heat until mixture comes away from base and side of saucepan and forms a smooth ball. Transfer mixture to small bowl; beat in egg with electric mixer until mixture becomes glossy.

3 Spoon mixture into piping bag fitted with 1cm plain tube. Pipe 5cm lengths of pastry mixture 3cm apart onto oven trays; bake 7 minutes. Reduce oven to 180°C/160°C fan-assisted; bake further 10 minutes or until éclairs are browned lightly and crisp. Carefully cut éclairs in half, remove any soft centre; bake further 5 minutes or until éclairs are dried out. Cool.

4 Spoon cream into piping bag fitted with 1cm plain tube; pipe cream onto 16 éclair halves; top with remaining halves. Place éclairs on foil-covered tray; spread with chocolate.

**tip** Fill the éclairs just before serving, you can have the éclair-tops already iced, ready for filling and joining.

# Low-fat chocolate ricotta tart

**preparation time** 15 minutes (plus refrigeration time) **cooking time** 35 minutes **serves** 8

¼ cup (35g) white self-raising flour

¼ cup (40g) wholemeal self-raising flour

2 tablespoons caster sugar

2 teaspoons cocoa powder

30g low-fat spread

2 teaspoons water

1 egg yolk

RICOTTA FILLING

150g low-fat ricotta

1 egg

1 egg yolk

¼ cup (70g) low-fat plain yogurt

¼ cup (55g) caster sugar

2 teaspoons white plain flour

2 tablespoons dark chocolate chips

2 teaspoons coffee-flavoured liqueur

1　Grease 18cm-round loose-based flan tin.

2　Process flours, sugar, sifted cocoa and spread until crumbly; add the water and egg yolk, process until ingredients just cling together. Knead dough gently on lightly floured surface until smooth, cover; refrigerate 30 minutes.

3　Preheat oven to 200°C/180°C fan-assisted.

4　Press dough into prepared tin; cover with baking parchment large enough to extend 5cm over edge, fill with dried beans or rice. Bake, on oven tray, 10 minutes; remove beans and paper. Bake further 5 minutes or until pastry is lightly browned; cool.

5　Reduce oven to 180°C/160°C fan-assisted. Make ricotta filling.

6　Pour ricotta filling into cooled tart case; bake, uncovered, about 20 minutes. Cool; refrigerate until firm.
　RICOTTA FILLING　Using electric mixer, beat ricotta, egg, egg yolk, yogurt, sugar and flour in medium bowl until smooth. Stir in chocolate chips and liqueur.

# Caramel chocolate tarts

**preparation time** 25 minutes (plus standing time)  **cooking time** 15 minutes  **makes** 24

1 cup (150g) plain flour
90g butter, chopped
¼ cup (55g) caster sugar
400g can sweetened condensed milk
30g butter, extra
2 tablespoons golden syrup
100g dark eating chocolate, melted

1 Preheat oven to 180°C/160°C fan-assisted. Grease two 12-hole 1½-tablespoon (30ml) mini-muffin pans.
2 Blend or process flour, butter and sugar until ingredients just come together. Press level tablespoons of butter mixture into each hole of prepared pans to form tart cases. Bake about 10 minutes or until browned lightly.
3 Meanwhile, combine condensed milk, extra butter and syrup in small saucepan; stir until smooth. Do not boil.
4 Pour hot caramel filling into hot cases; return to oven about 3 minutes or until caramel begins to brown around the edges. Stand 2 minutes; using a pointed vegetable knife, gently remove tarts from pans. Cool.
5 Spread top of cooled tarts with melted chocolate; stand until set.

**tip** The tarts can be made up to 3 days ahead. Refrigerate, covered, in an airtight container.

# Waffles with ice-cream & chocolate peanut sauce

**preparation time** 5 minutes  **cooking time** 5 minutes  **serves** 4

½ cup (125ml) double cream
2 x 60g Snickers™ bars, chopped coarsely
200g packaged waffles
vanilla ice-cream, for serving

1 Heat cream gently in a small saucepan, add Snickers™ bars and stir until melted and combined.
2 Toast waffles until crisp.
3 Divide waffles among serving plates or bowls, top with scoops of ice-cream and drizzle with sauce.

**tips** The sauce can be made several hours ahead; reheat gently. Sauce is suitable to microwave.

# Pear, chocolate & almond galettes

**preparation time** 5 minutes  **cooking time** 15 minutes  **makes** 4

80g dark eating chocolate, chopped finely

¼ cup (30g) ground almonds

1 sheet ready-rolled puff pastry, thawed

1 tablespoon milk

1 medium pear (230g)

1 tablespoon raw sugar

1  Preheat oven to 220°C/200°C fan-assisted. Line greased oven tray with baking parchment.

2  Combine chocolate and 2 tablespoons of the ground almonds in small bowl.

3  Cut pastry sheet into quarters; place quarters on oven tray, prick each with a fork, brush with milk. Divide chocolate mixture over pastry squares, leaving 2cm border.

4  Peel and core pear; cut into quarters. Cut each pear quarter into thin slices then spread one sliced pear quarter across each pastry square; sprinkle with sugar then remaining almond meal. Bake about 15 minutes.

**tip** A galette is a flattish kind of cake, originally from France, usually made from flaky pastry or yeast dough. This twist is easy and quick to do, but looks quite smart. All we've done is 'fan' the pear slices – you can do this with a lot of different types of fruit.

# Desserts

## Choc-brownies with caramel sauce

**preparation time** 10 minutes  **cooking time** 25 minutes  **serves** 6

80g butter, chopped

150g dark cooking chocolate, chopped coarsely

¾ cup (150g) firmly packed brown sugar

2 eggs, beaten lightly

1 teaspoon vanilla essence

¾ cup (110g) plain flour

300ml vanilla ice-cream

⅓ cup (45g) caramelised almonds, chopped coarsely

### CARAMEL SAUCE

⅔ cup (160ml) double cream

60g butter, chopped

¾ cup (150g) firmly packed brown sugar

1  Preheat oven to 220°C/200°C fan-assisted. Grease 6-hole large (¾ cup/180ml) muffin pan.

2  Combine butter, chocolate and sugar in medium saucepan; stir over medium heat until smooth.

3  Stir in egg, essence and flour; divide mixture among muffin pan holes. Cover pan tightly with foil; bake brownies about 20 minutes. Remove foil; stand 5 minutes.

4  Make caramel sauce.

5  Place brownies on serving plates; top with ice-cream, caramel sauce and caramelised almonds.

**CARAMEL SAUCE** Combine ingredients in small saucepan; stir over medium heat until smooth. Simmer 2 minutes.

**tip** The caramel sauce and chocolate-melting stage for the brownies can be done in a microwave oven.

# White chocolate fondue

preparation time 10 minutes  cooking time 5 minutes  serves 4

180g white eating chocolate, chopped coarsely

½ cup (125ml) double cream

1 tablespoon Malibu

1 cup (130g) fresh strawberries

1 large banana (230g), chopped coarsely

150g fresh pineapple, chopped coarsely

8 slices (35g) almond thins

16 marshmallows (100g)

1 Combine chocolate and cream in small saucepan, stir over low heat until smooth; stir in liqueur. Transfer fondue to serving bowl.

2 Place fondue in centre of dining table; serve remaining ingredients on a platter with skewers.

tip Fondue can be served with any of your favourite fruits.

# Chocolate nut bavarois with raspberry sauce

preparation time 30 minutes (plus refrigeration time)  cooking time 5 minutes  serves 6

1 cup (250ml) milk

½ cup (165g) chocolate hazelnut spread

4 egg yolks

¼ cup (55g) caster sugar

2 teaspoons gelatine

1 tablespoon water

300ml double cream

RASPBERRY SAUCE

200g fresh raspberries

2 tablespoons icing sugar

1 Combine milk and spread in small saucepan. Stir over heat until spread melts; bring to a boil. Transfer to medium bowl.

2 Beat egg yolks and caster sugar in small bowl with electric mixer until thick and creamy; gradually stir into chocolate mixture.

3 Sprinkle gelatine over the water in small heatproof jug; stand in small saucepan of simmering water, stirring, until gelatine dissolves. Stir gelatine mixture into warm chocolate mixture; cool to room temperature.

4 Beat cream in small bowl with electric mixer until soft peaks form; fold into chocolate mixture. Divide bavarois mixture among six ¾-cup (180ml) serving glasses; refrigerate about 4 hours.

5 Make raspberry sauce. Serve bavarois topped with raspberry sauce.
RASPBERRY SAUCE Push raspberries through sieve into small bowl; discard seeds. Stir in icing sugar.

tips If fresh raspberries are not available, use frozen raspberries, thawed.
As a guide, when dissolved gelatine is added to a mixture, both should be roughly the same temperature.

# Chocolate, pear & hazelnut self-saucing pudding

**preparation time** 30 minutes **cooking time** 1 hour 10 minutes **serves** 6

100g dark eating chocolate, chopped coarsely

50g butter, chopped

⅔ cup (160ml) milk

¼ cup (25g) ground hazelnuts

⅔ cup (100g) toasted hazelnuts, chopped coarsely

1 cup (220g) firmly packed brown sugar

1 cup (150g) self-raising flour

1 egg, beaten lightly

2 medium pears (460g)

300ml double cream

2 tablespoons icing sugar

2 tablespoons frangelico liqueur

FUDGE SAUCE

1¾ cups (430ml) water

100g butter, chopped

1 cup (220g) firmly packed brown sugar

½ cup (50g) cocoa powder, sifted

1 Preheat oven to 180°C/160°C fan-assisted. Grease shallow 3-litre (12-cup) baking dish.

2 Stir chocolate, butter and milk in small saucepan over low heat until smooth. Transfer to large bowl; stir in ground hazelnuts, nuts and brown sugar, then flour and egg.

3 Peel and core pears; slice thinly. Place pear slices, slightly overlapping, in prepared dish; top with chocolate mixture.

4 Make fudge sauce; pour over chocolate mixture. Bake, uncovered, about 1 hour. Stand 10 minutes.

5 Meanwhile, beat cream, icing sugar and liqueur in small bowl with electric mixer until soft peaks form. Serve pudding with frangelico cream.

FUDGE SAUCE Stir ingredients in small saucepan over low heat until smooth.

**tip** The frangelico can be omitted from the whipped cream mixture for an alcohol-free dessert.

# Minted white chocolate mousse

**preparation time** 10 minutes (plus standing and refrigeration time)  **cooking time** 5 minutes  **serves** 6

30g butter

120g white eating chocolate

2 egg whites

⅔ cup (160ml) whipping cream, whipped

green food colouring

2 teaspoons mint-flavoured liqueur

1 Melt butter in small saucepan or in microwave oven; stand 2 minutes. Skim off and reserve clarified butter from the top, leaving milky solids; discard solids.

2 Melt chocolate in medium heatproof bowl placed over a pan of simmering water (do not allow base of bowl to touch water); stir in clarified butter.

3 Beat egg whites in small bowl with electric mixer until soft peaks form. Gently fold egg white, cream and colouring into white chocolate mixture; stir in liqueur.

4 Divide mousse among serving glasses; refrigerate about 3 hours or overnight.

5 Decorate mousse with sliced strawberries and fresh mint leaves, if you like.

**tip** This mixture will make 2 cups mousse; you could also divide it among small glasses for serving. 40ml shot glasses will give you about 12 delicious mini servings.

# White chocolate ice-cream puddings

**preparation time** 20 minutes (plus cooling and freezing time)  **cooking time** 10 minutes  **makes** 8

1 vanilla pod

1¾ cups (430ml) milk

600ml double cream

180g white eating chocolate, chopped coarsely

8 egg yolks

¾ cup (165g) caster sugar

1 cup (130g) dried cranberries

2 tablespoons brandy

1 cup (140g) unsalted pistachios

2 teaspoons vegetable oil

1 Split vanilla pod lengthways; scrape seeds into medium saucepan. Add pod, milk, cream and 50g of the chocolate; bring to the boil.

2 Meanwhile, whisk egg yolks and sugar in medium bowl until thick and creamy; gradually whisk into hot milk mixture. Stir custard over low heat, without boiling, until thickened slightly. Cover surface of custard with cling film; cool 20 minutes.

3 Strain custard into shallow container, such as aluminium baking tin, cover with foil; freeze until almost firm.

4 Place ice-cream in large bowl, chop coarsely; beat with electric mixer until smooth. Pour into deep container, cover; freeze until firm. Repeat process two more times.

5 Meanwhile, place cranberries and brandy in small bowl; stand 15 minutes.

6 Stir cranberry mixture and nuts into ice-cream. Spoon ice-cream into eight ¾-cup (180ml) moulds. Cover, freeze 3 hours or until firm.

7 Stir remaining chocolate and oil in small saucepan over low heat until smooth.

8 Dip each mould, one at a time, into a bowl of hot water for about 1 second. Turn ice-creams onto serving plates; top with warm chocolate mixture.

# Chocolate soufflé with raspberry coulis

**preparation time** 15 minutes **cooking time** 20 minutes **serves** 4

1 tablespoon caster sugar

50g butter

1 tablespoon plain flour

200g dark eating chocolate, melted

2 egg yolks

4 egg whites

¼ cup (55g) caster sugar, extra

RASPBERRY COULIS

150g frozen raspberries, thawed

2 tablespoons caster sugar

4 cloves

½ cup (125ml) dry red wine

1 Preheat oven to 200°C/180°C fan-assisted. Grease four ¾-cup (180ml) soufflé dishes. Sprinkle insides of dishes evenly with sugar; shake away any excess. Place dishes on oven tray.

2 Melt butter in small saucepan, add flour; cook, stirring, about 2 minutes or until mixture thickens and bubbles. Remove from heat; stir in chocolate and egg yolks. Transfer to large bowl.

3 Beat egg whites in small bowl with electric mixer until soft peaks form. Gradually add extra sugar, one tablespoon at a time, beating until sugar dissolves between additions. Fold egg white mixture into chocolate mixture, in two batches.

4 Divide soufflé mixture among prepared dishes; bake, uncovered, about 15 minutes or until soufflés are puffed.

5 Meanwhile, make raspberry coulis.

6 Serve soufflés with raspberry coulis.
**RASPBERRY COULIS** Combine raspberries and sugar in small saucepan; cook, without boiling, until sugar dissolves. Add cloves and wine; bring to a boil. Reduce heat; simmer, uncovered, about 5 minutes or until coulis thickens. Strain coulis into medium jug.

# Chocolate mousse snowballs

**preparation time** 20 minutes (plus chilling and freezing time) **cooking time** 55 minutes **makes** 6

3 eggs

2½ tablespoons firmly packed brown sugar

240g dark eating chocolate, melted

⅔ cup (160ml) thick cream (48% fat)

2 tablespoons Cointreau

360g white eating chocolate, chopped coarsely

2 teaspoons vegetable oil

2 cups (100g) flaked coconut

1 Preheat oven to 180°C/160°C fan-assisted. Grease deep 15cm-round cake tin; line base and side with baking parchment.

2 Beat eggs and sugar in medium bowl with electric mixer until thick and creamy. Beat in cooled dark chocolate.

3 Fold in combined cream and liqueur; pour mixture into tin. Place pan in baking dish; pour enough boiling water into dish to come halfway up side of tin.

4 Bake cake 30 minutes. Cover loosely with foil; bake further 25 minutes. Cool cake in tin; refrigerate overnight.

5 Divide cake evenly into six wedges. Roll each wedge of cake into a ball, place on fine wire rack. Freeze balls about 1 hour or until firm.

6 Stir white chocolate and oil in small saucepan over low heat until smooth; cool 5 minutes. Spoon white chocolate mixture over balls to coat; freeze 5 minutes. Coat balls again with white chocolate mixture; roll in coconut. Refrigerate 20 minutes before serving.

# Dark chocolate ice-cream puddings

**preparation time** 30 minutes (plus cooling and freezing time) **cooking time** 10 minutes **serves** 6

*Candied clementines are available from
speciality food stores and delicatessens.*

1¾ cups (430ml) milk

600ml double cream

1 tablespoon cocoa powder

400g dark eating chocolate, chopped
coarsely

8 egg yolks

¾ cup (165g) caster sugar

2 tablespoons Cointreau

6 whole candied clementines

2 teaspoons vegetable oil

2 teaspoons cocoa powder

1 Combine milk, cream, sifted cocoa and 100g of the chocolate in medium saucepan; bring to the boil, stirring.

2 Meanwhile, whisk egg yolks and sugar in medium bowl until thick and creamy; gradually whisk into hot milk mixture. Stir custard over low heat, without boiling, until thickened slightly. Stir in liqueur. Cover surface of custard with cling film; cool 20 minutes.

3 Strain custard into shallow container, such as an aluminium baking tin, cover with foil; freeze until almost firm.

4 Place ice-cream in large bowl, chop coarsely, beat with electric mixer until smooth. Pour mixture into deep container, cover; freeze until firm. Repeat process two more times.

5 Line six 1-cup (250ml) moulds with cling film. Stand ice-cream at room temperature to soften slightly; spoon half of the ice-cream into the moulds. Using the back of a teaspoon, make a shallow hollow in the centre of ice-cream. Place one clementine in each hollow; top with remaining ice-cream. Smooth surface; cover, freeze 3 hours or until firm. Turn puddings onto a tray; return to freezer.

6 Cut six 14cm rounds from cling film or resealable bags. Stir remaining chocolate and oil in small pan over low heat until smooth. Spread melted chocolate over cling film then quickly drape plastic, chocolate-side down, over puddings. Quickly smooth with hands, to avoid making deep pleats in the plastic. Freeze until firm; peel away plastic. Serve ice-cream dusted with sifted cocoa.

# Chocolate berry meringues

**preparation time** 20 minutes (plus cooling time) **cooking time** 45 minutes **serves** 4

*If raspberries are not in season, you can vary the proportions of strawberries and blueberries to make a total of 550g.*

3 egg whites

¾ cup (165g) caster sugar

1 tablespoon cocoa powder

300ml whipping cream

150g fresh raspberries

250g fresh strawberries, quartered

150g fresh blueberries

1 Preheat oven to 120°C/100°C fan-assisted. Grease and line oven tray with baking parchment. Draw four 13cm-diameter circles on paper.

2 Beat egg whites in small bowl with electric mixer until soft peaks form. Add sugar, 1 tablespoon at a time, beating until sugar dissolves between each addition; fold in sifted cocoa.

3 Spread meringue mixture over drawn circles. Bake about 45 minutes or until firm; cool meringues in oven with door ajar.

4 Beat cream in small bowl with electric mixer until lightly whipped; top meringues with cream and berries.

**tip** When separating eggs, take care to avoid any yolk getting into the whites or they will not beat to the correct meringue consistency.

# White chocolate & strawberry cheesecake

**preparation time** 25 minutes (plus refrigeration time) **cooking time** 5 minutes **serves** 10

185g digestive biscuits

80g butter, melted

3 teaspoons gelatine

2 tablespoons water

500g cream cheese, softened

400g can sweetened condensed milk

300ml double cream

150g white eating chocolate, melted

500g large strawberries, hulled, halved

¼ cup (80g) strawberry jam, warmed, strained

1 tablespoon lemon juice

1 Grease 23cm springform cake tin.

2 Blend or process biscuits until mixture resembles fine breadcrumbs. Add butter; process until combined. Using hand, press biscuit mixture evenly over base of prepared tin, cover; refrigerate about 30 minutes or until firm.

3 Sprinkle gelatine over the water in small heatproof jug; stand jug in small saucepan of simmering water. Stir until gelatine dissolves. Cool 5 minutes.

4 Meanwhile, beat cheese and condensed milk in medium bowl with electric mixer until smooth. Beat cream in small bowl with electric mixer until soft peaks form.

5 Stir warm gelatine mixture into cheese mixture; fold in cream and chocolate. Pour cheesecake mixture into prepared tin, spreading evenly over biscuit base. Cover; refrigerate overnight.

6 Arrange strawberries on top of cheesecake; brush strawberries with combined jam and juice.

# Cookies & cream cheesecake

**preparation time** 20 minutes (plus refrigeration time) **cooking time** 5 minutes **serves** 12

*The first recorded mention of cheesecake dates all the way back to ancient Greece but it gained wide popularity in the Jewish delis of New York. Our version takes its flavour from the much-loved cookies and cream ice-cream variety.*

250g plain chocolate biscuits

150g butter, melted

2 teaspoons gelatine

¼ cup (60ml) water

360g cream cheese, softened

300ml double cream

1 teaspoon vanilla extract

½ cup (110g) caster sugar

180g white eating chocolate, melted

150g Oreo™ cookies, quartered

50g dark eating chocolate, melted

1  Line base of 23cm springform cake tin with baking parchment.
2  Blend or process plain chocolate biscuits until mixture resembles fine breadcrumbs. Add butter; process until just combined. Using hand, press biscuit mixture evenly over base and 3cm up side of prepared tin, cover; refrigerate 20 minutes.
3  Sprinkle gelatine over the water in small heatproof jug; stand jug in small saucepan of simmering water. Stir until gelatine dissolves; cool 5 minutes.
4  Beat cheese, cream, extract and sugar in medium bowl with electric mixer until smooth. Stir in gelatine mixture and white chocolate; fold in quartered cookies. Pour cheesecake mixture over biscuit base in tin, cover; refrigerate about 3 hours or until set. Drizzle with dark chocolate to serve.

**tip**  Place dark chocolate in a small plastic bag with the corner snipped off to help you drizzle it evenly over the cheesecake.

# Warm chocolate pavlovas

**preparation time** 5 minutes **cooking time** 35 minutes **serves** 4

2 egg whites

1⅓ cups (215g) icing sugar

⅓ cup (80ml) boiling water

1 tablespoon cocoa powder, sifted

500ml chocolate ice-cream

CHOCOLATE CUSTARD SAUCE

1 tablespoon cornflour

1 tablespoon cocoa powder, sifted

1 tablespoon caster sugar

1 cup (125ml) milk

2 egg yolks

1  Preheat oven to 180°C/160°C fan-assisted. Line large oven tray with baking parchment.
2  Beat egg whites, icing sugar and the water in small bowl with electric mixer about 10 minutes or until firm peaks form.
3  Fold sifted cocoa into meringue. Drop six equal amounts of mixture onto tray; use the back of a spoon to create well in centre of mounds. Bake about 25 minutes or until firm to touch.
4  Meanwhile, make chocolate custard sauce.
5  Serve pavlovas straight from the oven, topped with ice-cream and sauce.
   **CHOCOLATE CUSTARD SAUCE**  Blend cornflour, cocoa and sugar with milk in small saucepan. Stir in egg yolks. Stir over heat until sauce boils and thickens.

# Choc-hazelnut self-saucing puddings

preparation time 15 minutes  cooking time 25 minutes  serves 4

½ cup (125ml) milk

40g dark chocolate, chopped coarsely

50g butter

⅓ cup (35g) cocoa powder

½ cup (75g) self-raising flour

¼ cup (25g) ground hazelnuts

⅓ cup (75g) caster sugar

⅔ cup (150g) firmly packed brown sugar

1 egg, beaten lightly

¾ cup (180ml) water

40g butter, chopped, extra

200g vanilla ice-cream

CHOCOLATE HAZELNUT SAUCE

½ cup (125ml) double cream

2 tablespoons brown sugar

50g dark chocolate, chopped finely

⅓ cup (110g) chocolate hazelnut spread

1 tablespoon frangelico liqueur

1  Preheat oven to 180°C/160°C fan-assisted. Grease four 1-cup (250ml) ovenproof dishes.

2  Stir milk, chocolate, butter and half of the cocoa in small saucepan over low heat until smooth.

3  Combine flour, ground hazelnuts, caster sugar and half of the brown sugar in medium bowl. Add chocolate mixture and egg; stir until combined. Divide mixture among prepared dishes.

4  Stir the water, extra butter, remaining brown sugar and remaining cocoa in small saucepan over low heat until smooth. Pour hot mixture gently and evenly over puddings; bake puddings, uncovered, about 25 minutes. Stand 5 minutes.

5  Meanwhile, make chocolate hazelnut sauce.

6  Serve puddings topped with scoop of ice-cream and chocolate hazelnut sauce.

CHOCOLATE HAZELNUT SAUCE  Combine cream and sugar in small saucepan. Bring to a boil; remove from heat. Add chocolate; stir until smooth. Add spread and liqueur; stir until smooth.

tip  This dessert is best served hot because the sauce is quickly absorbed by the puddings.

desserts

# Soft-centred chocolate cakes with warm morello cherry sauce

**preparation time** 20 minutes  **cooking time** 15 minutes  **serves** 6

*Morello cherries have a dark mahogany-red skin and flesh and are slightly sour in taste. The combination of cherries and chocolate make this an irresistible dessert.*

185g dark chocolate, chopped coarsely

185g butter, chopped

3 egg yolks

⅓ cup (50g) plain flour

4 eggs

⅓ cup (75g) caster sugar

350g jar morello cherry jam

1 Preheat oven to 180°C/160°C fan-assisted. Grease six-hole large (¾-cup/180ml) muffin pan. Sprinkle with a little plain flour; tilt to coat holes, shake off any excess.

2 Place chocolate and butter in small saucepan; stir over low heat until mixture is smooth. Transfer to large bowl; stir in yolks and flour.

3 Beat eggs and sugar in small bowl with electric mixer about 5 minutes or until light and fluffy. Fold into chocolate mixture; spoon into prepared pan. Bake about 10 minutes; cakes should be soft in the centre. Stand 5 minutes; remove carefully from pan.

4 Meanwhile, melt jam in small saucepan over low heat; blend or process until smooth, strain. Return jam to saucepan, add a little water to give pouring consistency; bring to a boil. Skim surface; stand 5 minutes.

5 Serve warm soft-centred chocolate cakes drizzled with warm sauce.

**tip** Morello cherry jam can be found in most supermarkets.

# Chocolate bread & butter pudding

**preparation time** 20 minutes  **cooking time** 50 minutes  **serves** 6

*Rich egg-and-butter brioche can be made in the shape of a loaf or roll, but the most recognisable version is perhaps the 'brioche à tête' ('a roll with a head') that is formed by placing a small ball of dough on top of a larger one. One of France's first regional specialities, the brioche of Normandy dates back to the early 1400s.*

1½ cups (375ml) milk

2 cups (500ml) double cream

⅓ cup (75g) caster sugar

1 vanilla pod

4 eggs

2 small brioche (200g), sliced thickly

100g dark eating chocolate, chopped coarsely

⅓ cup (40g) coarsely chopped toasted pecans

1 Preheat oven to 180°C/160°C fan-assisted.

2 Combine milk, cream and sugar in small saucepan. Split vanilla pod in half lengthways; scrape seeds into pan, then place pod in pan. Stir over heat until hot; strain into large heatproof jug, discard pod.

3 Whisk eggs in large bowl; whisking constantly, add hot milk mixture.

4 Grease shallow 2-litre (8 cup) ovenproof dish; layer brioche, chocolate and nuts, overlapping brioche slightly, in dish. Pour hot milk mixture over top.

5 Place dish in large baking dish; add enough boiling water to come halfway up sides of dish. Bake, uncovered, about 45 minutes or until pudding sets. Remove pudding from baking dish; stand 5 minutes before serving.

# Runny chocolate fruit puddings

**preparation time** 20 minutes (plus freezing and cooling time) **cooking time** 12 minutes **serves** 6

160g bottled mincemeat

50g dark eating chocolate (70% cocoa solids), chopped coarsely

150g butter, chopped coarsely

3 eggs

⅓ cup (75g) firmly packed brown sugar

½ cup (75g) plain flour

¼ cup (35g) self-raising flour

1 tablespoon cocoa powder

CHOCOLATE RUM SAUCE

150g dark eating chocolate (70% cocoa solids), chopped coarsely

⅓ cup (80ml) double cream

2 tablespoons dark rum

1  Spoon mincemeat into 6 holes of a 1 tablespoon (20ml) ice cube tray; freeze for 3 hours.

2  Preheat oven to 200°C/180°C fan-assisted. Grease six 1-cup (250ml) pudding moulds.

3  Stir chocolate and butter in small saucepan over low heat until smooth. Cool 10 minutes.

4  Beat eggs and sugar in small bowl with electric mixer until thick and creamy; transfer mixture to medium bowl. Fold in sifted flours and cocoa, then chocolate mixture.

5  Spoon chocolate mixture into moulds. Remove frozen mincemeat cubes from tray; press one cube into centre of each pudding.

6  Bake puddings in preheated oven 12 minutes.

7  Meanwhile, make chocolate rum sauce. Serve puddings drizzled with sauce.
   **CHOCOLATE RUM SAUCE** Stir ingredients in small saucepan over low heat until smooth.

# Chocolate marquise

**preparation time** 30 minutes (plus refrigeration and freezing time)  **cooking time** 15 minutes  **serves** 10

*A marquise is based on the classic French bavarois (bavarian cream), a cold dessert composed of a rich egg custard, whipped cream and any of a number of flavourings, the choice being up to the cook – chocolate being our favourite. The chocolate sponge roll in this recipe is made with plain as opposed to self-raising flour because the beaten eggs are enough to aerate the mixture.*

¾ cup (180ml) double cream

100g dark eating chocolate, chopped coarsely

4 egg yolks

2 eggs

½ cup (110g) caster sugar

300ml double cream, extra

¼ cup (60ml) orange-flavoured liqueur

¾ cup (75g) coarsely grated dark eating chocolate

2 teaspoons finely grated orange rind

CHOCOLATE SPONGE

4 eggs

⅔ cup (150g) caster sugar

⅓ cup (50g) plain flour

1 tablespoon cocoa powder

1　Make chocolate sponge.

2　Line base and long sides of 14cm x 21cm loaf tin with baking parchment. Cut two rectangles from cooled sponge, one measuring 13cm x 21cm, the other 11cm x 19cm; discard remaining sponge.

3　Combine cream and chopped chocolate in small saucepan; stir over low heat until smooth. Beat egg yolks, eggs and sugar in medium bowl with electric mixer until thick and creamy; with motor operating, gradually beat hot chocolate mixture into egg mixture. Cover; refrigerate about 30 minutes or until mixture thickens slightly.

4　Meanwhile, beat extra cream in small bowl with electric mixer until soft peaks form; fold cream, liqueur, grated chocolate and rind into cooled chocolate mixture.

5　Place smaller rectangle of sponge in prepared tin; pour over chocolate mixture, top with remaining sponge rectangle. Cover with foil; freeze until firm. Turn marquise out onto board; stand at room temperature about 5 minutes or until softened slightly. Slice thickly, serve with fresh berries macerated in the same orange-flavoured liqueur, if desired.

CHOCOLATE SPONGE  Preheat oven to 180°C/160°C fan-assisted. Grease 25cm x 30cm swiss roll tin; line base with baking parchment. Beat eggs and sugar in small bowl with electric mixer until thick and creamy; transfer to large bowl. Fold in triple-sifted combined flour and cocoa; spread mixture into prepared tin. Bake, uncovered, about 10 minutes. Cool 10 minutes.

# Silky chocolate mousse

**preparation time** 15 minutes (plus cooling and refrigeration time) **cooking time** 5 minutes **serves** 8

300g dark eating chocolate, chopped coarsely

50g butter

3 eggs, separated

1 tablespoon irish cream liqueur

¼ cup (55g) caster sugar

300ml double cream, whipped

1 Combine chocolate and butter in small saucepan; stir over low heat until smooth. Remove from heat.

2 Stir in egg yolks, one at a time, then liqueur; transfer mixture to large bowl. Cool to room temperature.

3 Beat egg whites in small bowl with electric mixer until soft peaks form. Gradually add sugar, 1 tablespoon at a time, beating until sugar dissolves between each addition.

4 Meanwhile, fold cream into chocolate mixture, then fold in egg white mixture, in two batches. Divide chocolate mousse among eight ½-cup (125ml) serving dishes. Cover; refrigerate 2 hours or until set.

**tips** This mousse is best made a day ahead.
The chocolate and butter mixture is suitable to microwave.

# Berries with white chocolate sauce

**preparation time** **cooking time** 5 minutes **serves** 4

½ cup (125ml) double cream

125g white chocolate, chopped finely

1 tablespoon Malibu

500g fresh strawberries, quartered

300g fresh blueberries

1 Bring cream to a boil in medium saucepan; remove from heat. Add chocolate; stir until smooth. Stir in liqueur.

2 Serve warm sauce poured over berries.

# White chocolate, irish cream & berry trifle

**preparation time** 25 minutes (plus cooling and refrigeration time) **serves** 10

5 eggs

¾ cup (165g) caster sugar

500g mascarpone

300ml double cream

⅓ cup (25g) ground espresso coffee

2 cups (500ml) boiling water

1 cup (250ml) irish cream liqueur

2 x 250g packets sponge finger biscuits

75g white eating chocolate, grated

500g fresh strawberries, hulled

300g fresh raspberries

75g white eating chocolate, extra

1 Beat eggs and sugar in a medium bowl with an electric mixer about 10 minutes or until thick and creamy.

2 Beat mascarpone and cream in a large bowl with an electric mixer until thick. Fold egg mixture into mascarpone mixture.

3 Place coffee and boiling water in a coffee plunger; stand 2 minutes before plunging. Strain coffee through a fine sieve into a medium heatproof bowl; stir in liqueur.

4 Dip half of the biscuits, one at a time, briefly in coffee mixture until just starting to soften. Line the base of two shallow 2-litre (8 cup) or one 3.5-litre (14 cup) capacity serving dish with biscuits.

5 Spread half of the mascarpone mixture over the biscuits. Top with grated chocolate. Slice half of the strawberries and place over chocolate. Repeat layering process with remaining biscuits, coffee mixture and mascarpone mixture. Cover; refrigerate several hours or overnight.

6 Slice remaining strawberries; place on top of trifle with raspberries. Using a vegetable peeler, make chocolate curls from extra white chocolate. Sprinkle curls over berries just before serving.

**tip** This trifle is best made a day ahead.

# After-dinner treats

## Coconut ice-cream truffles

**preparation time** 15 minutes (plus freezing time)  **makes** 50

250ml vanilla ice-cream

2 teaspoons coconut-flavoured liqueur

1 tablespoon shredded coconut

125g plain sweet biscuits, crushed

400g white eating chocolate, melted

1¾ cups (135g) shredded coconut, extra

1 Combine slightly softened ice-cream, liqueur, coconut and biscuit in medium bowl. Cover with foil; freeze about 1 hour or until firm.

2 Working quickly, roll ½ level teaspoons of mixture into balls. Place on tray; freeze until firm.

3 Dip balls in melted chocolate; roll in extra coconut. Return to tray; freeze until firm.

### VARIATIONS

**hazelnut** Replace liqueur with 1 tablespoon chocolate hazelnut spread. Omit shredded coconut. Replace white chocolate with milk chocolate. Replace extra shredded coconut with 1½ cups finely chopped roasted hazelnuts.

**mocha walnut** Replace liqueur with 1 tablespoon strong black coffee. Omit shredded coconut. Replace white chocolate with dark chocolate. Replace extra shredded coconut with 1½ cups finely chopped roasted walnuts.

Coconut ice-cream truffles and
mocha walnut ice-cream truffles

# Chocolate cream fudge

**preparation time** 5 minutes (plus standing time)  **cooking time** 20 minutes  **makes** 49

*It is important to use a sugar thermometer in this recipe in order to get the correct consistency when making the fudge.*

1½ cups (330g) caster sugar

½ cup (100g) firmly packed brown sugar

60g dark cooking chocolate, chopped coarsely

2 tablespoons glucose syrup

½ cup (125ml) double cream

¼ cup (60ml) milk

40g butter

1  Grease deep 15cm-square cake tin.
2  Combine sugars, chocolate, syrup, cream and milk in small saucepan; stir over heat, without boiling, until sugar dissolves. Using pastry brush dipped in hot water, brush down side of pan to dissolve any sugar crystals; bring to a boil. Boil, uncovered, without stirring, about 10 minutes or until syrup reaches 116°C on sugar thermometer. Remove pan immediately from heat, leaving sugar thermometer in syrup; add butter, do not stir. Cool fudge about 20 minutes or until syrup drops to 40°C on sugar thermometer.
3  Stir fudge with wooden spoon about 10 minutes or until a small amount dropped from the spoon holds its shape. Spread fudge into prepared pan; cover with foil. Stand at room temperature about 3 hours or until fudge sets. Turn fudge out of pan; trim edges. Cut into 2cm squares.

# Mint choc bites

**preparation time** 20 minutes  **cooking time** 30 minutes  **makes** 36

125g butter, chopped

200g dark eating chocolate, chopped coarsely

½ cup (110g) caster sugar

2 eggs, beaten lightly

1¼ cups (185g) plain flour

1½ cups (240g) icing sugar

1 teaspoon butter, extra

¼ teaspoon peppermint essence

2 tablespoons milk, approximately

50g dark chocolate, melted, extra

1  Preheat oven to 180°C/160°C fan-assisted. Grease deep 19cm-square cake tin; line base with baking parchment.
2  Combine butter and chocolate in medium saucepan; stir over low heat until chocolate melts. Stir in caster sugar and egg, then flour. Spread mixture into prepared tin; bake about 20 minutes. Stand cake in tin 15 minutes; turn onto wire rack to cool.
3  Meanwhile, combine icing sugar, extra butter and essence in small heatproof bowl; gradually stir in enough milk to make mixture form a thick paste. Stir mixture over small saucepan of simmering water until icing is of spreadable consistency. Spread icing over cake; set at room temperature.
4  Using serrated knife, trim crisp edges from cake. Cut cake into 3cm squares; drizzle each square with extra chocolate.

# Snickers rocky road

**preparation time** 15 minutes (plus refrigeration time)  **cooking time** 5 minutes  **makes** 54 squares

*We have taken a traditional rocky road recipe and given it a new look by adding Snickers™ bars and toasted, rather than plain, marshmallows.*

4 x 60g Snickers™ bars, chopped coarsely

1 cup (35g) rice crispies

150g toasted marshmallows, chopped coarsely

1 cup (150g) toasted unsalted peanuts

400g milk eating chocolate, chopped coarsely

2 teaspoons vegetable oil

1  Grease 19cm x 29cm baking tin. Line base and two long sides with baking parchment, extending paper 2cm above sides of pan.

2  Combine Snickers™, rice crispies, marshmallows and nuts in large bowl. Stir chocolate and oil in small saucepan over low heat until smooth. Cool 5 minutes.

3  Pour chocolate mixture into Snickers™ mixture; mix until well combined. Spoon rocky road mixture into prepared tin; refrigerate, covered, about 30 minutes or until set. Remove from tin, trim edges of mixture; cut into 3cm squares. Store, covered, in the refrigerator.

# Gourmet rocky road

**preparation time** 20 minutes (plus refrigeration time)  **makes** 40 slices

300g toasted marshmallows, chopped coarsely

400g turkish delight, chopped coarsely

¼ cup (40g) toasted blanched almonds, chopped coarsely

½ cup (75g) toasted shelled pistachios

450g white eating chocolate, melted

1  Grease two 8cm x 26cm baking tins; line base and sides with baking parchment, extending paper 5cm above long sides.

2  Combine marshmallows, turkish delight and nuts in large bowl. Working quickly, stir in chocolate; spread mixture into prepared pans, push mixture down firmly to flatten the top. Refrigerate until set, then cut as desired.

# White choc, citrus & coconut truffles

**preparation time** 40 minutes (plus refrigeration time)  **cooking time** 5 minutes  **makes** 30

½ cup (125ml) coconut cream
2 teaspoons finely grated lime rind
2 teaspoons finely grated lemon rind
360g white eating chocolate, chopped coarsely
1¼ cups (85g) shredded coconut

1  Combine coconut cream, rinds and chocolate in small saucepan; stir over low heat until smooth. Transfer mixture to small bowl, cover; refrigerate 3 hours or overnight.
2  Working with a quarter of the chocolate mixture at a time (keeping remainder refrigerated), roll rounded teaspoons into balls; place on tray. Refrigerate truffles until firm.
3  Working quickly, roll truffles in coconut, place in mini patty pans on tray; refrigerate until firm.

# Dark chocolate & ginger truffles

**preparation time** 40 minutes (plus refrigeration time)  **cooking time** 5 minutes  **makes** 30

⅓ cup (80ml) double cream
200g dark eating chocolate, chopped coarsely
½ cup (115g) glacé ginger, chopped finely
¼ cup (25g) cocoa powder

1  Combine cream and chocolate in small saucepan; stir over low heat until smooth, stir in ginger. Transfer to small bowl, cover; refrigerate 3 hours or overnight.
2  Working with a quarter of the chocolate mixture at a time (keeping remainder refrigerated), roll rounded teaspoons into balls; place on tray. Refrigerate truffles until firm.
3  Working quickly, roll balls in cocoa, place in mini patty pans on tray; refrigerate truffles until firm.

# Cranberry, port & dark choc truffles

**preparation time** 40 minutes (plus refrigeration time) **cooking time** 5 minutes **makes** 30

¼ cup (60ml) whipping cream

200g dark eating chocolate, chopped coarsely

2 tablespoons port

⅓ cup (50g) dried cranberries, chopped coarsely

300g dark eating chocolate, melted

1  Combine cream and chopped chocolate in small saucepan; stir over low heat until smooth, stir in port and cranberries. Transfer to small bowl, cover; refrigerate 3 hours or overnight.

2  Working with a quarter of the chocolate mixture at a time (keeping remainder under refrigeration), roll rounded teaspoons into balls; place on tray. Freeze truffles until firm.

3  Working quickly, dip truffles in melted chocolate then roll gently in hands to coat evenly, return to tray; refrigerate until firm.

# Peanut butter & milk choc truffles

**preparation time** 40 minutes (plus refrigeration time) **cooking time** 5 minutes **makes** 30

⅓ cup (80ml) whipping cream

200g milk eating chocolate, chopped coarsely

¼ cup (70g) unsalted crunchy peanut butter

¾ cup (110g) crushed peanuts

1  Combine cream and chocolate in small saucepan; stir over low heat until smooth, stir in peanut butter. Transfer to small bowl, cover; refrigerate 3 hours or overnight.

2  Working with a quarter of the chocolate mixture at a time (keeping remainder under refrigeration), roll rounded teaspoons into balls; place on tray. Refrigerate truffles until firm.

3  Working quickly, roll balls in peanuts, return to tray; refrigerate truffles until firm.

# Choccy orange sticks

preparation time 25 minutes (plus standing time) cooking time 20 minutes makes 48

2 large thick-skinned oranges (600g)

1 cup (220g) caster sugar

1 cup (250ml) water

200g dark eating chocolate, melted

1 Cut oranges into quarters. Peel away skin, leaving pith attached to skin. Cut skin with pith into 1cm-thick strips; discard fruit.

2 Drop orange strips into pan of boiling water, return to a boil; drain. Repeat twice.

3 Combine sugar and the water in medium saucepan. Stir over heat, without boiling, until sugar dissolves. Add orange strips; bring to a boil. Reduce heat; simmer, uncovered, stirring occasionally, about 5 minutes or until strips become translucent.

4 Meanwhile, place wire rack over baking-parchment-lined tray.

5 Remove strips from syrup with tongs; place on wire rack in single layer. Dry, uncovered, overnight.

6 Line tray with baking parchment. Using dipping forks or skewers, dip strips, one at a time, into melted chocolate; place on tray. Allow to set at room temperature.

# White chocolate & pistachio truffles

preparation time 15 minutes (plus refrigeration time) cooking time 5 minutes makes 8

1½ tablespoons double cream

60g white eating chocolate, chopped coarsely

¼ cup (35g) unsalted pistachios, chopped finely

1 teaspoon coconut-flavoured liqueur

120g white eating chocolate, chopped coarsely, extra

1 tablespoon finely chopped unsalted pistachios, extra

1 Combine cream and chocolate in small heatproof bowl; stir over small saucepan of simmering water until smooth (do not let water touch base of bowl). Remove bowl from pan, stir in nuts and liqueur. Cover; refrigerate until firm.

2 Roll level teaspoons of mixture into balls, place on baking-parchment-lined tray. Cover; refrigerate until firm.

3 Stir extra chocolate in small heatproof bowl over small saucepan of simmering water until smooth (do not let water touch base of bowl). Remove bowl from pan. Dip chocolate balls into melted chocolate, place on baking-parchment-lined tray; sprinkle with extra nuts. Cover; refrigerate until firm.

# Choc-orange ricotta dates

**preparation time** 20 minutes (plus standing time)  **makes** 10

10 large fresh dates
1 tablespoon orange-flavoured liqueur
½ cup (120g) ricotta cheese
1 tablespoon icing sugar
1 teaspoon finely grated orange rind
50g dark eating chocolate, melted

1  Make a shallow slit lengthways in each date;
   remove stones. Combine dates and liqueur in
   medium bowl; stand 15 minutes.
2  Meanwhile, combine cheese, sifted icing sugar
   and rind in small bowl with wooden spoon.
3  Drain liqueur from dates into cream cheese
   mixture; stir until combined. Place dates on wire
   rack. Spoon cream cheese mixture into piping
   bag; pipe mixture into dates.
4  Drizzle dates with melted chocolate; allow to
   set at room temperature.

# Chocolate marzipan almonds

**preparation time** 35 minutes (plus refrigeration time)  **cooking time** 10 minutes  **makes** 30

30 (40g) whole blanched almonds
200g marzipan or almond paste
125g dark eating chocolate, melted

1  Preheat oven to 180°C/160°C fan-assisted.
2  Roast nuts in single layer on oven tray about
   5 minutes or until golden brown; cool.
3  Mould level teaspoons of paste around each
   nut. Place on wire rack; stand, uncovered,
   overnight, until dry to touch.
4  Using dipping forks or skewers, dip each nut
   into chocolate. Place nuts on foil-lined tray;
   allow to set at room temperature.

# Rich chocolate truffles

**preparation time** 20 minutes (plus standing time)  **cooking time** 5 minutes (plus cooling time)  **makes** 20

200g dark chocolate, chopped coarsely
2 tablespoons double cream
1 tablespoon Cointreau
⅓ cup (35g) cocoa powder

1  Combine chocolate and cream in medium heatproof bowl over medium saucepan of barely simmering water; stir until smooth. Remove from heat; cool. Stir in liqueur. Cover; stand at room temperature 3 hours or until firm.
2  Roll 2 level teaspoons of the mixture into balls. Place sifted cocoa in medium bowl. Toss balls to coat in cocoa; shake away excess cocoa. Refrigerate truffles in an airtight container.

**tip** This recipe can be made a week ahead; roll truffles in cocoa 3 hours before serving.

# Chocolate twists

**preparation time** 15 minutes  **cooking time** 10 minutes  **makes** 24

1 sheet ready-rolled puff pastry
2 tablespoons apple juice
100g milk eating chocolate, melted

1  Preheat oven to 200°C/180°C fan-assisted. Line oven tray with baking parchment.
2  Cut pastry in half. Cut each half crossways into 2cm strips.
3  Place juice in small bowl. Dip pastry strips into juice, one at a time; twist each strip, place, in single layer, on tray. Bake about 10 minutes or until pastry is golden brown.
4  Dip one end of each pastry twist into melted chocolate, return to tray to set.

after-dinner treats

# Macaroons with chocolate drizzle

**preparation time** 30 minutes  **cooking time** 10 minutes  **makes** 28

1 egg white

⅔ cup (150g) caster sugar

¼ teaspoon almond extract

1 cup (125g) ground almonds

½ cup (70g) toasted slivered almonds, chopped coarsely

50g dark eating chocolate, melted

1 Preheat oven to 180°C/160°C fan-assisted. Lightly grease and line two oven trays.

2 Beat egg white in small bowl with electric mixer until soft peaks form. Gradually add sugar, 1 tablespoon at a time, beating until sugar dissolves between additions. Transfer egg-white mixture to medium bowl; fold in extract, ground almonds and nuts.

3 Divide mixture in half; roll each half into 20cm log. Cut each log into 14 pieces; roll each piece into 6cm log. Place logs on prepared trays; bake, uncovered, about 8 minutes. Cool on trays; drizzle or pipe macaroons with melted chocolate.

# Triple chocolate fudge

**preparation time** 30 minutes (plus cooling and refrigeration time)  **cooking time** 10 minutes  **makes** 50

1½ cups (330g) caster sugar

½ cup (110g) firmly packed brown sugar

100g dark eating chocolate, chopped coarsely

2 tablespoons glucose syrup

½ cup (125ml) double cream

¼ cup (60ml) milk

40g butter

200g white eating chocolate, melted

50g milk eating chocolate, melted

1 Grease and line an 8cm x 26cm baking tin with baking parchment, extending paper 2cm above the sides of the pan.

2 Stir sugars, dark chocolate, syrup, cream and milk in small saucepan over heat, without boiling, until sugars dissolve. Bring to the boil; boil without stirring, about 10 minutes or until mixture reaches 116°C on sugar thermometer. Remove pan immediately from heat, leaving thermometer in mixture; add butter, do not stir.

3 Cool fudge about 40 minutes or until mixture drops to 40°C. Remove thermometer. Stir fudge with wooden spoon about 10 minutes or until a small amount dropped from spoon holds its shape. Spread fudge into baking tin; smooth surface. Cover with foil; stand at room temperature 2 hours.

4 Spread white chocolate over fudge, drizzle with milk chocolate. Pull a skewer through the chocolate topping for a marbled affect. Refrigerate fudge for 3 hours or overnight.

5 Remove fudge from tin, cut in half lengthways before slicing thinly.

# Glossary

**almonds**
**blanched** skins removed.
**caramelised** toffee-coated almonds.
**essence** often interchangeable with extract; made with almond oil and alcohol or another agent.
**flaked** paper-thin slices.
**ground** also known as almond meal; nuts are powdered to a coarse flour texture.
**slivered** cut lengthways.
**bicarbonate of soda** also called baking soda.
**brioche** rich French yeast-risen bread made with butter and eggs. Available from pâtisseries or specialty bread shops.
**buttermilk** fresh low-fat milk cultured to give a slightly sour, tangy taste; low-fat yogurt or milk can be substituted.
**cashews** plump, kidney-shaped, golden-brown nuts with a distinctive sweet, buttery flavour and containing about 48 per cent fat. Because of this high fat content, they should be kept, sealed tightly, under refrigeration to avoid becoming rancid. We use roasted unsalted cashews in this book, unless otherwise stated; they're available from health-food stores and most supermarkets.
**chocolate**
**chips** available in milk, white and dark chocolate. Made of cocoa liquor, cocoa butter, sugar and an emulsifier, these hold their shape in baking and are ideal for decorating.
**dark cooking** we used premium quality dark cooking chocolate rather than compound.
**dark eating** made of cocoa liquor, cocoa butter and sugar.
**drinking** sweetened cocoa powder.
**hazelnut spread** we use Nutella.

It was originally developed when chocolate was hard to source during World War II; hazelnuts were added to extend the chocolate supply.
**milk eating** most popular eating chocolate, mild and very sweet; similar in make-up to dark, but with the addition of milk solids.
**white eating** contains no cocoa solids, deriving its sweet flavour from cocoa butter. Is very sensitive to heat.
**cinnamon** dried inner bark of the shoots of the cinnamon tree. Available as a stick or ground.
**cloves** can be used whole or in ground form. Has a strong scent and taste so should be used minimally.
**cocoa powder** also known as unsweetened cocoa; cocoa beans that have been fermented, roasted, shelled, ground into powder then cleared of most of the fat content.
**coconut**
**desiccated** unsweetened and concentrated, dried finely shredded.
**flaked** dried flaked coconut flesh.
**milk** not the juice found inside the fruit, which is known as coconut water, but the diluted liquid from the second pressing from the white meat of a mature coconut (the first pressing produces coconut cream). Available in cans and cartons at supermarkets.
**shredded** thin strips of dried coconut.
**coffee-flavoured liqueur** we use either Kahlua or Tia Maria coffee-flavoured liqueur.
**cointreau** orange-flavoured liqueur.
condensed milk a canned milk product consisting of milk with more than half the water content removed and sugar added to the milk that remains.
**cornflour** also known as cornstarch. Available made from corn or wheat

(wheaten cornflour, gluten-free, gives a lighter texture in cakes); used as a thickening agent in cooking.
**cranberries, dried** have the same slightly sour, succulent flavour as fresh cranberries. Can usually be substituted for or with other dried fruit in most recipes. Available in most supermarkets. Also available in sweetened form.
**cream** we used fresh cream in this book, unless otherwise stated. Also known as pure cream and pouring cream; has no additives unlike commercially thickened cream. Minimum fat content 35 per cent.
**soured** a thick commercially-cultured soured cream. Minimum fat content 35 per cent.
**whipping** a cream that contains a thickener. Has a minimum fat content of 35 per cent.
**cream cheese** a soft cow's-milk cheese with a fat content ranging from 14 per cent to 33 per cent.
**custard powder** instant mixture used to make pouring custard; similar to North American instant pudding mixes.
**dark rum** we prefer to use an underproof rum (not overproof) for a more subtle flavour.
**date** fruit of the date palm tree, eaten fresh or dried, on their own or in prepared dishes. About 4cm to 6cm in length, oval and plump, thin-skinned, with a honey-sweet flavour and sticky texture.
**drambuie** whisky-based liqueur.
**figs** small, soft, pear-shaped fruit with a sweet pulpy flesh full of tiny edible seeds. Vary in skin and flesh colour according to type, not ripeness; when ripe, figs should be unblemished and bursting with flavour; nectar beads at

the base indicate when a fig is at its best. Figs may also be glacéd, dried or canned in sugar syrup.

**flour**
**plain** all-purpose flour, made from wheat.
**self-raising** plain flour sifted with baking powder (a raising agent consisting mainly of 2 parts cream of tartar to 1 part bicarbonate of soda) in the proportion of 150g flour to 2 level teaspoons baking powder.
**wholemeal** flour milled with the wheat germ so is higher in fibre and more nutritional than plain flour.
**food colouring** vegetable-based substance available in liquid, paste or gel form.
**frangelico** hazelnut-flavoured liqueur.
**gelatine** we used powdered gelatine; also available in sheet form known as leaf gelatine.

**ginger**
**glacé (or stem)** fresh ginger root preserved in sugar syrup. Crystallised ginger can be substituted if rinsed with warm water and dried before using.
**ground** also known as powdered ginger; used as a flavouring in cakes, pies and puddings but cannot be substituted for fresh ginger.
**glacé cherries** also known as candied cherries; boiled in heavy sugar syrup and then dried. Used in cakes, breads and sweets.
**glacé fruit** fruit such as cherries, peaches, pineapple, orange and citron cooked in heavy sugar syrup then dried.
**glucose syrup** also known as liquid glucose, made from wheat starch; used in jam and confectionery and available at health food stores and supermarkets.
**golden syrup** a by-product of refined sugarcane; pure maple syrup or honey can be substituted.
**hazelnuts** also known as filberts; plump, grape-size, rich, sweet nut

with a brown inedible skin that can be easily removed by rubbing heated nuts together vigorously in a tea towel.
**ground** meal made by grinding hazelnuts to a coarse flour texture for use in baking or as a thickening agent.
**irish cream liqueur** we used Baileys, a smooth and creamy blend of fresh Irish cream, the finest Irish spirits, Irish whiskey, cocoa and vanilla.
**kirsch** cherry-flavoured liqueur.
**macadamias** native to Australia, a rich and buttery nut; store in refrigerator because of its high oil content.
**malibu** a coconut-flavoured rum.
**marshmallows** pink and white; made from sugar, glucose, gelatine and cornflour.
**mixed peel** candied citrus peel.
**mixed spice** a blend of ground spices usually consisting of cinnamon, allspice and nutmeg.
**nutmeg** dried nut of an evergreen tree; available in ground form or you can grate your own using a fine grater.
**orange-flavoured liqueur** you can use any orange-flavoured liqueur: Grand Marnier, Cointreau, Curaçao are all suitable.
**peanut butter** peanuts ground to a paste; available in crunchy and smooth varieties.
**pecans** native to the United States; golden-brown, buttery and rich. Good in savoury and sweet dishes; especially good in salads.
**pistachios** pale green, delicately flavoured nut inside hard off-white shells. To peel, soak shelled nuts in boiling water about 5 minutes; drain, then pat dry.
**polenta** a flour-like cereal made of ground corn (maize); similar to cornmeal but finer and lighter in colour; also the name of the dish made from it.
**prunes** commercially or sun-dried plums; store in the fridge.

**rice paper** an edible, translucent paper made from a dough of water combined with the pith of an Asian shrub. The fine, glossy paper is edible and is very useful in the making of biscuits, such as macaroons. It is not eaten uncooked.
**ricotta** a soft, sweet, moist, white, cow's-milk cheese with a low fat content (about 8.5 per cent) and a slightly grainy texture. The name roughly translates as 'cooked again' and refers to ricotta's manufacture from a whey that is itself a by-product of other cheese making.

**sugar**
**brown** an extremely soft, fine granulated sugar retaining molasses for its deep colour and flavour.
**caster** also known as superfine or finely granulated table sugar.
**icing** also known as confectioners' sugar or powdered sugar.
**raw** natural brown granulated sugar.

**vanilla**
**essence** obtained from vanilla beans infused in alcohol and water.
**extract** obtained from vanilla beans infused in water; a non-alcoholic version of essence.
**pod** dried long, thin pod from a tropical golden orchid grown in central and South America and Tahiti; the minuscule black seeds inside the bean are used to impart a distinctively sweet vanilla flavour. A whole pod can be placed in a container of sugar to make vanilla sugar.
**walnuts** cream-coloured, wrinkled nuts with brown skin, formed into two distinct halves.
**white vinegar** made from spirit of cane sugar.
**yeast** allow 2 teaspoons (7g) dried yeast to each 15g compressed yeast if substituting.
**yogurt** an unflavoured, full-fat cow's-milk yogurt has been used in these recipes unless stated otherwise.
**low-fat** we used yogurt with a fat content of less than 0.2 per cent.

# Index

# Conversion charts

## measures

The cup and spoon measurements used in this book are metric: one measuring cup holds approximately 250ml; one metric tablespoon holds 20ml; one metric teaspoon holds 5ml.

All cup and spoon measurements are level. The most accurate way of measuring dry ingredients is to weigh them. When measuring liquids, use a clear glass or plastic jug with the metric markings.

We use large eggs with an average weight of 60g. This book contains recipes for dishes made with raw or lightly cooked eggs. These should be avoided by vulnerable people such as pregnant and nursing mothers, invalids, the elderly, babies and young children.

## dry measures

| METRIC | IMPERIAL |
| --- | --- |
| 15g | ½oz |
| 30g | 1oz |
| 60g | 2oz |
| 90g | 3oz |
| 125g | 4oz (¼lb) |
| 155g | 5oz |
| 185g | 6oz |
| 220g | 7oz |
| 250g | 8oz (½lb) |
| 280g | 9oz |
| 315g | 10oz |
| 345g | 11oz |
| 375g | 12oz (¾lb) |
| 410g | 13oz |
| 440g | 14oz |
| 470g | 15oz |
| 500g | 16oz (1lb) |
| 750g | 24oz (1½lb) |
| 1kg | 32oz (2lb) |

## liquid measures

| METRIC | IMPERIAL |
| --- | --- |
| 30ml | 1 fluid oz |
| 60ml | 2 fluid oz |
| 100ml | 3 fluid oz |
| 125ml | 4 fluid oz |
| 150ml | 5 fluid oz (¼ pint/1 gill) |
| 190ml | 6 fluid oz |
| 250ml | 8 fluid oz |
| 300ml | 10 fluid oz (½ pint) |
| 500ml | 16 fluid oz |
| 600ml | 20 fluid oz (1 pint) |
| 1000ml (1 litre) | 1¾ pints |

## length measures

| METRIC | IMPERIAL |
| --- | --- |
| 3mm | ⅛ in |
| 6mm | ¼in |
| 1cm | ½in |
| 2cm | ¾in |
| 2.5cm | 1in |
| 5cm | 2in |
| 6cm | 2½in |
| 8cm | 3in |
| 10cm | 4in |
| 13cm | 5in |
| 15cm | 6in |
| 18cm | 7in |
| 20cm | 8in |
| 23cm | 9in |
| 25cm | 10in |
| 28cm | 11in |
| 30cm | 12in (1ft) |

## oven temperatures

These oven temperatures are only a guide for conventional ovens. For fan-assisted ovens, check the manufacturer's manual.

| | °C (CELSIUS) | °F (FAHRENHEIT) | GAS MARK |
| --- | --- | --- | --- |
| Very low | 120 | 250 | ½ |
| Low | 150 | 275-300 | 1-2 |
| Moderately low | 160 | 325 | 3 |
| Moderate | 180 | 350-375 | 4-5 |
| Moderately hot | 200 | 400 | 6 |
| Hot | 220 | 425-450 | 7-8 |
| Very hot | 240 | 475 | 9 |

This book is published by Octopus Publishing Group Limited based on materials licensed it by ACP Magazines Ltd, a division of PBL Media Pty Limited

54 Park St, Sydney
GPO Box 4088, Sydney, NSW 2001
phone (02) 9282 8618;
fax (02) 9267 9438
acpbooks@acpmagazines.com.au;
www.acpbooks.com.au

OCTOPUS BOOKS

Design: Chris Bell
Food Director: Pamela Clark

Published and Distributed in the United Kingdom by Octopus Publishing Group Limited

Endeavour House
189 Shaftesbury Avenue
London WC2H 8JY
United Kingdom
phone + 44 (0) 207 632 5400;
fax + 44 (0) 207 632 5405

aww@octopusbooks.co.uk; www.octopusbooks.co.uk
www.australian-womens-weekly.com

Printed and bound in China

International foreign language rights,
Brian Cearnes, ACP Books
bcearnes@acpmagazines.com.au

A catalogue record for this book is available from the British Library.

ISBN 978-1-907428-02-9
© ACP Magazines Ltd 2010
ABN 18 053 273 546

To order books:
telephone LBS on 01903 828 503
order online at www.australian-womens-weekly.com
or www.octopusbooks.co.uk

# THE MUTED GLEAM OF ANTIQUE

The spirit of classicism is one of disciplined elegance: discreet rather than flamboyant. In this boldly coloured interior, our Classic Collection motifs give an unobtrusive richness to a disparate collection of pieces. It is the details that score here. Note how strikingly the painted borders set off the coloured picture mounts, and how a discreet use of gold lining and ornament gives status to a very ordinary small dining table. Gilt wreaths dramatize the seats of plain painted wooden chairs, while the matching

# GOLD

carver sports a glamorous flowering lyre. For
contrast, compare the metallic effects with the same
designs painted in white on the tray table. Two
borders combined with lining make something quite
splendid from a deep, moulded mirror frame,

glimpsed hanging just above. Strongly coloured walls
and the black woodwork dado rail create a dramatic
decorative scheme with an Arts and Crafts
atmosphere that is currently one of the top favourites
with younger interior designers.

# PAINTING WITH A PATTERN

*Small repeat motifs decorating a simple shape make an ideal project to test your skills.*

Our stylized fleur-de-lys motif makes a reassuringly easy project to start with, as well as adding considerable visual impact to the wooden jardiniere.

Points to remember:
- Use a hard lead pencil for the tracing down because this will give you a clear outline.
- Keep a clean copy of the tracing patterns - you might like to photocopy them a few times. You can then cut them up to fit awkward spaces without worrying about losing the originals.
- Background colours throughout this pattern book

were achieved with standard emulsion paints, applied over either acrylic primer or thoroughly sanded existing paint.
- Many of the designs were painted with the gold version of artists' gouache in tubes, available from all good artists' suppliers. Artists' acrylic tube colour, fast-drying and convenient, was used for painting in coloured details. Gilt lining becomes simplicity itself done with a ruler and a gold felt pen.
- The beauty of these timeless motifs is that they somehow look appropriate on most simply shaped pieces from any period. Interpreting them in gold

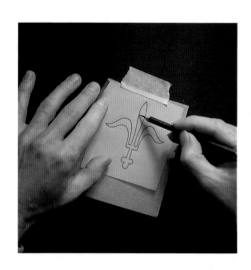

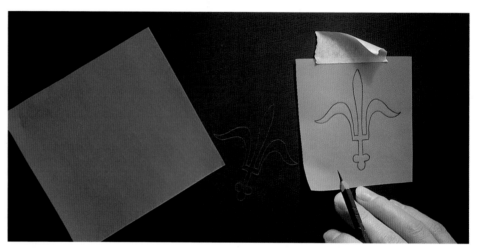

*1* A TAB OF MASKING TAPE HOLDS THE TRACING PATTERN IN PLACE OVER THE BLUE TRANSFER PAPER, WHILE THE PATTERN IS TRACED DOWN FIRMLY WITH A WELL-SHARPENED HARD LEAD PENCIL.

*2* THIS SHOWS THE COMPLETED MOTIF TRANSFERRED TO THE PAINTED SURFACE USING OUR BLUE TRANSFER PAPER. TO MAKE THE JOB EASIER, USE A SMALL SQUARE OF TRANSFER PAPER THAT HAS BEEN CUT TO THE DIMENSIONS OF THE MOTIF.

*3* USING A MEDIUM-SIZED WATERCOLOUR BRUSH AND COLOUR A, FILL IN THE FLEUR-DE-LYS PETALS STARTING AT THEIR EXTREMITIES FOR A CLEAN AND DECISIVE POINT. PRACTISE THIS BRUSHWORK IF YOU LIKE ON A PIECE OF PAPER FIRST.

*4* WITH A CLEAN BRUSH DIPPED IN COLOUR B, HIGHLIGHT THE PETALS AS SHOWN. USE YOUR FREE HAND TO SUPPORT THE PAINTING HAND WHILE YOU WORK.

*5* MORE GOLD GOUACHE IS USED TO HIGHLIGHT THE TREFOIL SHAPE AT THE BASE OF OUR MOTIF.

MATERIALS CHECKLIST

WELL-SHARPENED HARD LEAD PENCIL, SCISSORS, MASKING TAPE, OLD
PLATE, WATER JAR, KITCHEN PAPER OR TISSUES FOR WIPING BRUSHES,
RULER OR TAPE FOR POSITIONING MOTIFS.

ACRYLIC TUBE COLOURS IN VENETIAN RED, ALIZARIN CRIMSON AND
HOOKER'S GREEN.

GOLD FELT PEN.

GOUACHE TUBE COLOUR IN GOLD.

TWO WATERCOLOUR BRUSHES, ONE FINE, ONE MEDIUM.

LENGTH OF BULL-NOSED MOULDING FOR LINING WITH GOLD FELT PEN
OR FINE BRUSH.

COLOUR RECIPES:

(A) ALIZARIN CRIMSON MIXED WITH A VERY LITTLE VENETIAN RED.
(B) GOUACHE GOLD THINNED WITH WATER.

against dark paintwork creates an effect reminiscent
of Empire furniture with its severe shapes brightened
by ormolu, brass stringing and touches of gold leaf.
• Use soft watercolour brushes in different sizes to
outline and fill in motifs. There is no need to buy
expensive sable brushes - synthetic bristles or mixed
hair are fine.

*1* THIS SHOWS THE ANTHEMION DESIGN
MOTIF TRACED OFF USING BLUE TRANSFER
PAPER. EVEN AGAINST A DARK BACKGROUND
LIKE THE ONE HERE, THE OUTLINES ARE QUITE
CLEAR ENOUGH TO REGISTER.

*2* A GOLD FELT PEN MAKES A DELIGHTFULLY
SIMPLE PAINTING TOOL, AS SHOWN HERE.
NOTE HOW A WHISKER OF BACKGROUND
COLOUR LEFT VISIBLE GIVES VIVACITY TO THE
STYLIZED PETAL SHAPES.

*3* SIGNING OFF THE COMPLETED MOTIF. THE
ANTHEMION SHAPE IS A TRADITIONAL
ORNAMENT OFTEN USED IN COMBINATION
WITH GOLD LINES TO DECORATE THE CORNERS
OF PIECES OF FURNITURE.

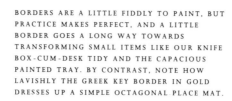

BORDERS ARE A LITTLE FIDDLY TO PAINT, BUT PRACTICE MAKES PERFECT, AND A LITTLE BORDER GOES A LONG WAY TOWARDS TRANSFORMING SMALL ITEMS LIKE OUR KNIFE BOX-CUM-DESK TIDY AND THE CAPACIOUS PAINTED TRAY. BY CONTRAST, NOTE HOW LAVISHLY THE GREEK KEY BORDER IN GOLD DRESSES UP A SIMPLE OCTAGONAL PLACE MAT.

COLOUR RECIPES:
(A) GOUACHE WHITE THINNED WITH WATER.
(B) ALIZARIN CRIMSON MIXED WITH A VERY LITTLE VENETIAN RED.

*1* A BULL-NOSED (ROUNDED) MOULDING MAKES PAINTING A FINE STRAIGHT LINE EASIER, STEADYING THE BRUSH HAND AND PREVENTING PAINT SMUDGING AS IT MIGHT IF YOU USED A FLAT RULER. USE A FINE BRUSH FOR THIS WITH COLOUR A.

*2* HAVING ESTABLISHED THE CENTRE LINE, THE SAME COLOUR AND BRUSH ARE USED TO FILL IN WHITE DOTS - WHICH REPRESENT BERRIES - BEFORE CHANGING TO A CLEAN BRUSH AND COLOUR B TO FILL IN THE TRACED-DOWN LEAF SHAPES.

*3* THE FINISHED BORDER HAS A CRISP ELEGANCE THAT HAS MADE IT A FAVOURITE DECORATIVE DEVICE SINCE THE DAYS OF CLASSICAL GREEK VASE PAINTING.

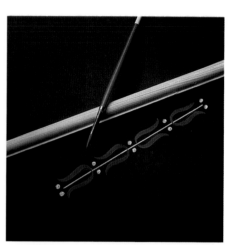

*1* THE BEVELLED EDGE OF A STANDARD PLASTIC SET SQUARE WORKS WELL AS AN AID TO LINING WITH A GOLD FELT PEN. TRY TO MAINTAIN EVEN PRESSURE, TAKING SPECIAL CARE OVER 'JOINS'. PRACTISE FIRST ON A SHEET OF PAPER TO GET THE HANG OF IT.

*2* WITH THE OUTER LINES IN PLACE, DRAWING OUT THE REST OF THIS CLASSIC SCROLL BORDER IS RELAXING AND SPEEDY, SIMPLY A CASE OF 'GOING OVER' THE TRACED-DOWN DESIGN.

*3* THE GOLD FELT PEN AGAIN IS AN IDEAL TOOL FOR EXECUTING THIS VARIANT ON THE SCROLL BORDER MOTIF. BUT, AS BEFORE, IT ALWAYS HELPS TO REHEARSE THE MOVEMENTS FIRST ON ROUGH PAPER BECAUSE CONFIDENCE BREEDS FLUENCY.

OUR TRANSFER APPROACH ALLOWS BEGINNERS TO ACHIEVE LIVELY BUT RELAXED EXECUTION OF TRADITIONAL BORDER MOTIFS LIKE THE ONES SHOWN ON THIS PAGE. NOTE: ANY GOLD FELT PEN DECORATION NEEDS 'FIXING' WITH SPRAY VARNISH BEFORE ANY FURTHER SEALING OR VARNISHING.

*1* THE CELEBRATED GREEK KEY BORDER, STILL THE MOST ARRESTING OF GEOMETRIC MOTIFS, BEGINS HERE WITH TRACING DOWN THE BORDER ELEMENTS THROUGH BLUE TRANSFER PAPER USING A SHARP PENCIL.

*2* FILLING IN THE DESIGN AS SHOWN HERE, WITH SHORT DASHES AND RETAINING OUTER GUIDELINES, SPEEDS UP THE REPETITIVE ELEMENT WHICH IS AN INEVITABLE PART OF HAND-PAINTED BORDERS.

*3* THE FINAL AND FUN BIT, YET AGAIN, CONSISTS OF FILLING IN THE MISSING ELEMENTS WITH THE GOLD FELT PEN USING THE BLUE TRACINGS AS A GUIDE.

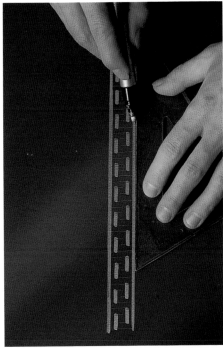

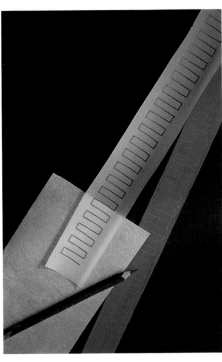

*1* A CONTINUOUS GOLD LINE MAKES A HANDSOME AND EFFECTIVE BORDER DEVICE, ESPECIALLY STRIKING WHEN, AS HERE, IT IS SET OFF BY A CONTRASTING PAINTED BAND, USING COLOUR MIX B.

*2* FOR SPEED AND ACCURACY, USE THE BULL-NOSED MOULDING TO GUIDE THE SHORT DASH STROKES. YOU NEED TO MAINTAIN A STRAIGHT LINE IF THIS SIMPLE MOTIF IS TO KEEP TO THE STRAIGHT AND NARROW.

*3* WITH GUIDELINES ESTABLISHED, IT IS EASY AND STRAIGHTFORWARD TO FILL IN THE MISSING SECTIONS OF THE BORDER MOTIF TO CREATE A CONTINUOUS LINE. THE FELT PEN TECHNIQUE IS ESPECIALLY HELPFUL FOR EXECUTING DESIGNS WITH LOTS OF ANGLES.

*Two of the most poetic images of antiquity - the laurel wreath and the flowering lyre - make superb decorations for a space where a strong shape is needed like the chair seats shown here.*

COLOUR RECIPE:
(A) GOLD GOUACHE TUBE COLOUR.

1 MEDIUM AND FINE BRUSHES ARE BEING USED WITH COLOUR A TO FILL IN THE LEAVES AND BERRIES OF THE WREATH MOTIF. NOTE HOW THE DARK BACKGROUND 'GHOSTING' THROUGH CONTRIBUTES TO THE SUBTLY SHADED EFFECT.

2 THE WREATH HAS BEEN BLOCKED IN LEAVING PLENTY OF DARK SHADOWING. NOW CAREFULLY PAINT IN THE ELABORATELY FLUTTERING BOW RIBBONS USING THE FINE BRUSH.

3 STRENGTHEN HIGHLIGHTS THROUGHOUT THE MOTIF BY STIPPLING MORE PAINT ONTO LEAVES AND RIBBON WITH THE POINT OF THE BRUSH, CREATING A DELICATE AND CONTROLLED BUILD-UP OF COLOUR.

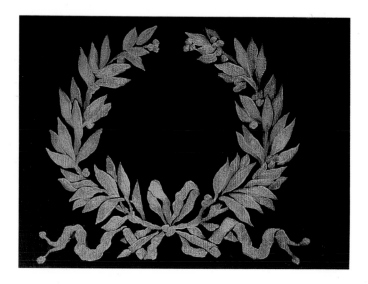

4 THE FINISHED MOTIF HAS A ROMANTIC, PAINTERLY QUALITY THAT WOULD ENHANCE ANY SUITABLY CLASSICAL PIECE. IMAGINE IT ON A CHAIR BACK, CENTRING A ROUND TABLE TOP OR ON A DOOR PANEL.

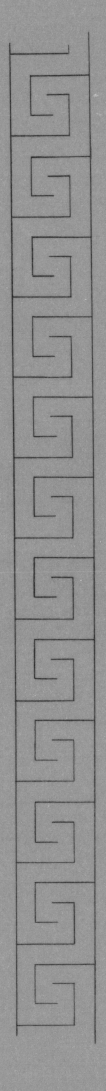

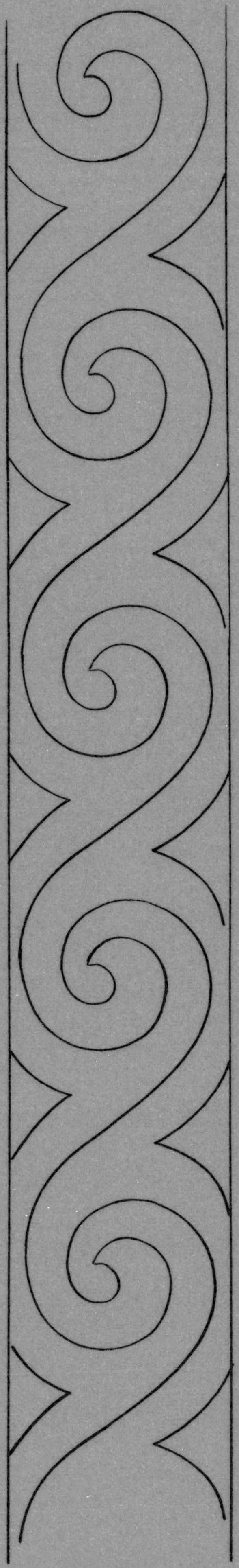

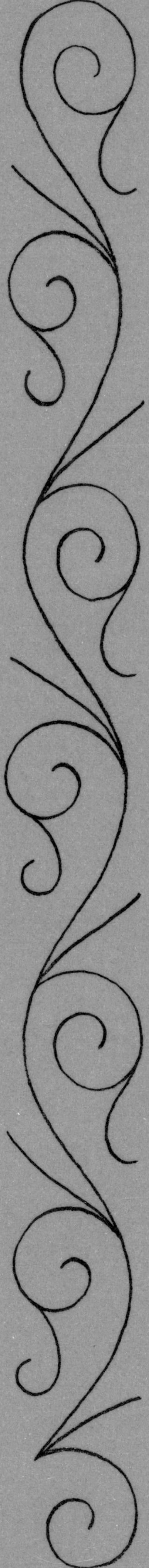

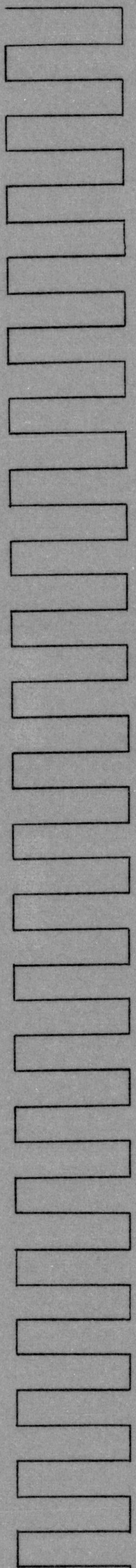

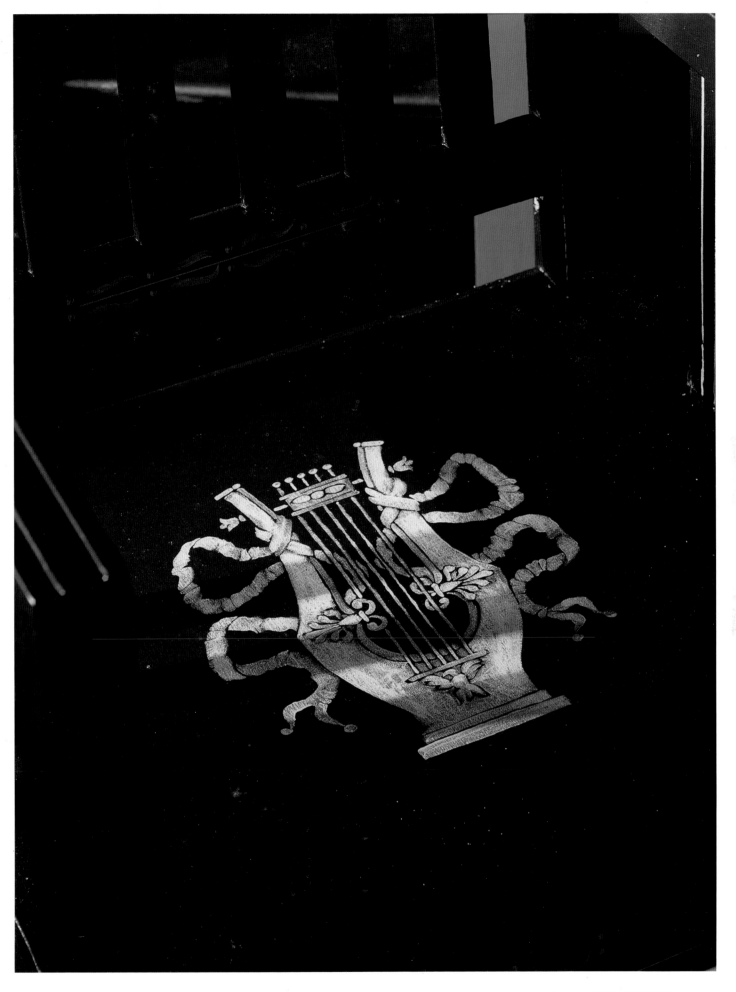

OUR VERSION OF THE NEO-
CLASSICAL FLOWERING LYRE MOTIF
MAKES ANOTHER STRIKING AND
GLAMOROUS ORNAMENT, STRONG
ENOUGH TO STAND ALONE WITH
PERHAPS A LITTLE GILT LINEWORK
AS A FRAME.

*Glossy dark colours and painted ornament combine for Empire elegance.*

# PAINT PROTECTION

The reason designers keep going back to the classical vocabulary of ornament is that these motifs manage to be both adaptable and timeless. Use them scaled up for drama, or discreetly, as here, adding style and shapeliness to simple pieces. Details like the ones highlighted are quick to do with our transfers but they create a strong visual link and can be the making of a room.

PIECES THAT GET A LOT OF USE AND WEAR LIKE THIS TABLE NEED THOROUGH FINISHING TO KEEP PAINT AND DECORATION IN GOOD SHAPE. APPLY AT LEAST TWO COATS OF CLEAR GLOSS POLYURETHANE VARNISH. RUB THE FINAL COAT WITH FINE WET-AND-DRY ABRASIVE PAPER DIPPED INTO WATER. THIS GIVES A LUXURIOUSLY SILKY FINISH WITH GOOD PROTECTION FOR WHAT IS UNDERNEATH.

ALWAYS GIVE GOLD FELT PEN WORK A QUICK BLAST OF SPRAY VARNISH TO 'FIX' IT BEFORE GOING ON TO FURTHER TREATMENTS; OTHERWISE THERE IS A RISK OF SMUDGING THE PEN WORK WHEN THE SURFACE IS BRUSHED.

SPLENDID EXAMPLES OF THE ELEGANCE OF CLASSIC BORDERS TRANSFORMING THE MOST BASIC SHAPES: THIS SET OF DARK GREEN PLACE MATS AND THE SIDES OF A WELL-PROPORTIONED TRAY DON THE GREEK KEY AND SCROLL MOTIFS. ON PIECES LIKE THESE, LIKELY TO BE SUBJECTED TO HEAVY DAILY USE, CAREFUL AND THOROUGH VARNISHING IS ESPECIALLY IMPORTANT TO PROTECT YOUR WORK.

# DECORATIVE DETAILS THAT TRANSFORM A ROOM

*Use our classic motifs to give a touch of class quickly and easily to all sorts of household items.*

THIS STRIKING QUARTET OF FRAMED PRINTS SHOWS HOW EFFECTIVELY FELT PEN WORK CAN UPGRADE THE CHEAPEST FRAMES. THE SECRET IS IN THE PICTURE MOUNTS: PLAIN CARD IN BLACK AND WHITE, BUT GIVEN TERRIFIC IMPACT BY RICHLY COLOURED BANDS OF DECORATION ENCLOSING THE PICTURE SPACE. TO SUGGEST SOME OF THE POTENTIAL FOR VARIATION, COMPARE THE DECORATION ON THE TWO SMALLER FRAMES, WHERE THE IDENTICAL GREEK KEY BORDER IS GIVEN A QUITE DIFFERENT LOOK BY ALTERING THE BACKGROUND COLOURS AND USING A BLACK FELT PEN ON ONE AND A GOLD PEN ON THE OTHER. WHEN THE FRAMING LOOKS THIS DISTINGUISHED AND CONFIDENT, YOU CAN GET AWAY WITH MERE PHOTOCOPIES OF PICTURES, AS WE DID HERE.

A STRONG COLOUR SCHEME LIKE THIS POMPEIIAN-INSPIRED USE OF WARM DARK COLOURS TEMPERED WITH BLACK GIVES AN INTERIOR IMMENSE CHARACTER. BUT TERRACOTTA WALLS COULD FEEL CLAUSTROPHOBIC WITHOUT PICTURES TO CREATE 'WINDOWS' WITHIN THE WALL SURFACE. OUR FOUR PICTURES HAVE BEEN HUNG SYMMETRICALLY ACROSS THE WALL. THE PALE MOUNTS ON THE LARGER FRAMES BALANCE THE BLACK PAINTED FIREPLACE BELOW, AND THE COLOURED BANDS ON ALL FOUR MOUNTS PICK UP AND ENHANCE COLOURS ALREADY PRESENT ELSEWHERE IN THE ROOM.

ADAPT YOUR DECORATIVE IDEAS TO THE
SHAPE AND STYLE OF YOUR PAINTED
PIECES. THIS UPRIGHT CARVER-STYLE
CHAIR HAS BEEN DECORATED TO FOCUS
INTEREST ON THE BACK AND SEAT. THE
GLAMOROUS LYRE MOTIF ON THE SEAT IS
BALANCED BY SIMPLE GILT LINES AND
DOTS ON THE BACK UPRIGHTS, AND A
SMALL SNIPPET OF A BORDER DESIGN ON
THE FRONT RAIL.

THIS REPRO VERSION OF A CLASSIC PIECE OF
FURNITURE – THE TEA OR DRINKS TRAY ON A
FOLDING STAND – HAS BEEN GIVEN A CHIC
PERIOD LOOK BY PAINTING IT GLOSSY BLACK
AND UNDERLINING ITS SHAPE WITH
DECORATION IN PLAIN WHITE.

*More changes to ring on a classic theme.*

GOLD PEN WORK AND BANDS OF CONTRAST
COLOUR RELATED TO THE ROOM'S COLOUR
SCHEME MAKE A RATHER HEAVY OLD PICTURE
MOULDING INTO A MIRROR FRAME WITH REAL
DECORATIVE IMPACT. THE ENTIRE FRAME WAS
FIRST PAINTED, AND THEN RAISED SECTIONS
WERE DRAMATIZED WITH GOLD PEN WORK
BORDERS. FINALLY, THE INNER BEVELLED EDGE
WAS PAINTED OVER IN GOLD GOUACHE PAINT.

A SMART LIVERY OF BLACK AND GOLD SUITS
THIS SLENDER STANDARD LAMP, AN
INEXPENSIVE JUNK-SHOP FIND, ITS CHIC
ACCENTUATED BY A PLAIN BLACK SHADE.
GOLD LINES CIRCLING THE BASE AND
STEM DRAW ATTENTION TO THE LAMP'S
GRACEFUL SHAPE, AS WELL AS CUTTING
THE 'BEANPOLE' LOOK DOWN TO SIZE.

WITH A LITTLE THOUGHT AND
IMAGINATION YOU CAN GET MORE
MILEAGE FROM ANY MOTIF. THE
ANTHEMION DESIGN USED IN A RING-A-
ROSY CIRCLE AROUND THE LAMP BASE IS
ONE EXAMPLE OF INTELLIGENT
ADAPTATION THAT HAS TURNED OUT
TRIUMPHANTLY WELL.